AMERICA

TURNING A NATION TO GOD

TONY EVANS

Moody Publishers

CHICAGO

All Scripture quotations, unless otherwise indicated, are taken from the *New American Standard Bible®*. Copyright ©1960, 1962, 1963, 1968, 1971, 1972, 1973, 1975, 1977, 1995 by The Lockman Foundation. Used by permission. (www.Lockman.org)

Scripture quotations marked (NIV) are taken from the Holy Bible, New International Version®, NIV®. Copyright © 1973, 1978, 1984, 2011 by Biblica, Inc.™ Used by permission of Zondervan. All rights reserved worldwide. www.zondervan.com. The "NIV" and "New International Version" are trademarks registered in the United States Patent and Trademark Office by Biblica, Inc.™

Scripture quotations marked KJV are taken from the King James Version.

Edited by Jim Vincent
Interior design: Ragont Design
Author photo: Trey Hill
Cover design: Design Corps
Cover photo of American flag copyright © 2007 Lafotoguy/iStock 3981396. All rights reserved.

Chapter 6 is adapted from the booklet *Tony Evans Speaks Out on Fasting* (Chicago: Moody, 2000).

Portions of chapter 11 first appeared in Tony Evans, *Are Christians Destroying America?* (Chicago: Moody, 1996), chapter 2.

Library of Congress Cataloging-in-Publication Data

Evans, Tony, 1949-
America : turning a nation to God / by Tony Evans.
  pages cm
 Summary: "Dr. Tony Evans not only examines the root of our nation's social, economic, and political unrest but presents a plan for reclaiming freedom, morality, and strength. We hold within the collective body of Christ not only the power but also the capacity to put our country back on the path of ascendancy. This straightforward teaching, when embraced by believers in our nation, will usher in the greatest revival in American history"-- Provided by publisher.
Includes bibliographical references.
ISBN 978-0-8024-1267-6 (hardback)
1. United States—Religion. 2. Christianity—United States. 3. United States—Social conditions—21st century. 4. United States—Economic conditions—21st century. 5. Church renewal—United States. 6. Religious awakening—United States. 7. Revivals—United States. I. Title.
BR517.E93 2015
269.0973--dc23
                         2014037147

All websites and phone numbers listed herein are accurate at the time of publication, but may change in the future or cease to exist. The listing of website references and resources does not imply publisher endorsement of the site's entire contents. Groups and organizations are listed for informational purposes, and listing does not imply publisher endorsement of their activities.

We hope you enjoy this book from Moody Publishers. Our goal is to provide high-quality, thought-provoking books and products that connect truth to your real needs and challenges. For more information on other books and products written and produced from a biblical perspective, go to www.moodypublishers.com or write to:

Moody Publishers
820 N. LaSalle Boulevard
Chicago, IL 60610

1 3 5 7 9 10 8 6 4 2

Printed in the United States of America

CONTENTS

INTRODUCTION

The Crisis We Face

America is in serious trouble. From sea to shining sea we are witnessing the devolution of a nation. Regardless of which side of the political aisle you sit, it is clear that things are unraveling at warp speed. The United States is quickly becoming the divided states as signs of disunity and conflicts abound. From family breakdowns to the immigration crisis to the abiding racial divide to Congress' inability to function, it is clear we are a fraying nation. Add to this the continuing moral decay that is engulfing us, whether it is the redefinition of marriage and the family, abortions on demand, a media that continues to dumb down decency, or an educational system that increasingly seeks to impart information without ethics in the name of "freedom." We are as a nation sliding south fast.

At the same time, the constant threat of terrorism and an overblown debt threaten not only our economic future, but the future of our children and grandchildren as well.

The American dream is quickly becoming the American nightmare as more and more citizens become disillusioned with the direction things seem to be going.

As people gather unofficially around the water cooler at work—or officially around government sanctioned summits, seeking to find solutions to the myriad of issues that plague us— real long-term answers continue to elude us.

In the midst of all of this, God's church seems to be of little help in giving real answers to real problems in spite of the proliferation of Christian literature, programming, and facilities. In fact, the Christian faith and its symbols are more marginalized than ever.

There are only two explanations before us as we witness what is happening to our beloved nation. Either we are on the verge of the completion of an eschatology calendar that will usher in the return of Christ to judge the earth and set up His earthly kingdom, or we are enduring the passive wrath of God whereby He allows a person or a society to experience the consequences of their rejection of Him. The more people marginalize the true God of the Bible the more chaotic things become.

However, such judgment opens the door for revival when God's church returns to Him in humility and repentance. The return of Christ is outside of our hands, but revival and its social and cultural benefits are very much in our hands. Even when the church has become an unintentional co-conspirator in the culture's demise through its compromise with the culture, it can be empowered when it turns about to God in repentance.

That is what this book is about. It is a call for America to turn to God in hopes that He will reverse our course and restore our union to His definition of what a nation is to be when it operates under His rule. Such a restoration must be led by His church; for God will not skip the church house in order to change the White House (Ephesians 3:10).

God and His rule is America's only hope; and the church operating under His authority is the means for the realization of that hope, since it alone has been given the keys of the kingdom (Matthew 16:18–19). It is my prayer that God will use this book to encourage, inspire, and challenge believers in Christ to become kingdom disciples through whom our God can work to bring revival to His church and through it, to our land.

Tony Evans

Dallas, Texas

PART 1

Returning to the King

1

When the King Is Your Problem

S he was just a girl. A young teen—fourteen years old in a society and a day dominated by men. The year was 1904 and it was Valentine's Day. She sat in a chapel in Wales, having only been converted to Jesus Christ not long before.

Tremors of political, social, and economic unrest rumbled beneath the surface of her nation. Many of its citizens spent their days digging in mines for coal, hands and hearts darkened by the soot and blackness surrounding them. They wasted their wages on liquor, their leisure on pleasure. Women had few rights at that time, and fourteen-year-old girls nearly none.

Regardless, God is no respecter of humanity's value systems. God values all and will use whomever He chooses to carry out His work, usually someone we would least expect.

Like fourteen-year-old Florrie Evans, whom some called Flo.

As history credits Rosa Parks for starting the American Civil Rights Movement, history also credits Florrie Evans as starting one of the greatest national revivals of all time, a revival that ultimately spread internationally as well—impacting us here in America.

The Valentine's Day service was part of a two-month series of meetings where Pastor Joseph Jenkins had been preaching on themes of revival, renewal, and turning to God. During the morning's service, Pastor Jenkins opened the floor up for testimonies on spiritual life and power. Young men stood to talk one by one but each time they rambled off topic, so Pastor Jenkins asked them to sit back down. One by one, these young men sat down, exhaling an air of timidity that infected the hearts of the others still seated.

"I Love Jesus . . . with *All* My Heart."

Who else would stand when the pastor kept telling everyone to sit back down before they had even finished? Who else, but Florrie.

The fourteen-year-old stood to her feet after a long duration of silence, and with voice trembling she said these simple words: "I love Jesus Christ—with *all* my heart."

Those in attendance have testified that at that moment they witnessed a change in the atmosphere. It is reported that as she spoke those words, the Holy Spirit's presence and power fell upon the meeting—the air and the attendees, even the timid young men. So impactful was that moment that many, if not most, historians credit it, and this young girl, as the beginning of the 1904 Welsh Revival. Her words would influence a church and a nation. Her opening and only sentence began a spiritual renewal that would usher in thousands of new believers, reduce the tavern sales in one Welch town to only nine cents on a Saturday night, cure alcoholics, lower crime, and increase justice and equality in the political realm. It would spread the fire of the Holy Spirit across the nations and even the world.[1]

What Florrie Evans is identified with starting, Evan Roberts—a Welch preacher at that time—is attributed as continuing. Days before

Florrie's simple statement, Evan had felt compelled to increase his time in daily prayer from several hours a day to seven. God had placed a burden on his heart for a spiritual awakening in his land and around the world. The number 100,000 burned in his mind. He believed that was the number God was going to bring to spiritual salvation in his country through a time of national renewal.

A GOVERNMENT TRANSFORMED

Roberts continued to pray until God began anointing his preaching in such a way that the Spirit's power flooded those in attendance. Services would often run until 3 a.m. Others soon joined Evan in proclaiming the message, men and women alike, and the movement spread.

Within less than a year after Florrie's proclamation, and as Evan's preaching led the way, 100,000 people had come to the Lord. But not only that, the government had been transformed—in fact, judges began wearing white gloves to symbolize the change. The national systems were reformed, churches filled to overflowing. Families were strengthened. And the movement of God's Spirit spread across the oceans to nations near and far.

You can be certain an awakening is authentic when even the secular news media joins in. The *London Times* began writing of the happenings as a regular, and positive, update in their paper. On January 1, 1905, they quoted the pastor of Saint John's Wood Presbyterian Church as saying, "The mighty and unseen breath of the Spirit was doing in a month more than centuries of legislation could accomplish."

On January 10, *The Times* wrote that, "for the first time there was not a single case of drunkenness at the Swansea Petty Sessions." The next day, a *Times* reporter quoted Parliament member David Lloyd George as saying, "At the next election Wales would declare with no uncertain sound against the corruption in high places that handed over the destiny of the people to the horrible brewing interest." David Lloyd

George went on to become the British prime minister (1916–22).

The Welsh awakening lasted a year but its effects resounded for decades. Real transformation and change was seen and experienced not only in Wales, but around the world. All because one young girl, Florrie Evans, was brave enough to stand and confess Christ publicly, while a preacher named Evan Roberts pleaded to the Lord and proclaimed the message of the Holy Spirit to his nation.

Never underestimate the power of a person. Never underestimate the power of prayer. Never underestimate the power of proclamation. Never underestimate the Lord.

Friends and fellow citizens, the turmoil, corruption, inequity, and distress we are experiencing in our nation today can be addressed. It can be reversed. We can be transformed. Will it take humbling ourselves before the Lord? Yes. Will it take concerted and united prayer? Yes. Will it take an awakening in the body of Christ? Yes. But all of these things are possible if we will return to God's Word, and make His principles and precepts the basis for our lives, and when we seek both His face and the Holy Spirit on behalf of ourselves, our families, our churches, and our land.

Nothing is ever too out of reach that God cannot revive it.

Nothing is ever too out of reach that God cannot revive it. Yet in order to *turn* our nation to God, we—His people—will need to make a collective effort to *return* to Him first.

Revivals do not happen spontaneously. Awakenings do not happen unknowingly. Rather, they are first conceived in people's hearts, then fed through prayer and fasting, which then gives birth to the organization of and call for localized and collective solemn assemblies, thus giving way to lasting transformation.

It is time for a birth like this in our land.

THE HISTORIC SOLEMN ASSEMBLY

When a solemn assembly or sacred gathering was called in Scripture, it was often called by those in leadership—whether that be a priest, prophet, or king.[2] Often it would first be called for a specific smaller leadership sphere before spreading to the entire nation. Even in America, our historical records verify that prior to every national awakening, the spiritual leadership of the day placed a heavy emphasis on fasting and gathering for times of solemn assemblies, typically in smaller groups that then led to larger gatherings.

During the inception of revival, God will often speak to people in separate locations, giving them the similar vision of the need for this type of gathering. When leaders and people meet who may not see each other often, or even know each other, they find that conversations turn to God's movement within their hearts. As a result, a synergy arises among denominations and leadership. And people who may have never worked together across church, denominational, or organizational lines now have their paths cross in this one overarching purpose.

A solemn assembly for the purpose of restoration is a sacred gathering where God's people, during a specific time of fasting and prayer, seek the renewal of their relationship with Him through the repentance of sin and the passionate pursuit of the return of His presence in their midst. It can also be defined as *a specific movement of God, by His Holy Spirit, through His leadership where He gathers the saints to Himself.*

Biblical history is replete with this similar theme of the assembling of the saints and God's subsequent restoration. After all, God has a heart for reconciliation. From the garden in Genesis to the heavens in Revelation, God issues a call time and again for reconciliation prior to announcing judgment. He is swift to spare, if we will but ask Him for the new heart and the new spirit as His prescribed pathway to seeing hope restored and lives transformed (Ezekiel 18:30–31).

OF CICADAS AND LOCUSTS

Never walk under a tree during a cicada emergence. I learned that early while growing up in Baltimore. Cicadas (who many misname as locusts) suck the juice of trees for their food. After eating they will, well—let me just say that they don't keep it all in and you don't want to be standing under them when they don't.

More helpful advice: Be careful when using a lawn mower during a cicada emergence. Cicadas confuse the sound of the mower with that of other cicadas. So they'll land on you—by the dozens. And plucking them off is akin to removing the spots off a leopard. Godspeed if you try. You'll need it.

And be wary if your neighbor offers a "special" sandwich or "special" pie during the cicadas' emergence as well. People have been known to barbecue, boil, bake, and fry these critters that mob by the millions during their seventeenth-year cycle of mating.

Cicada swarms have wreaked havoc throughout our world and throughout all time. When China was set to host the Beijing Olympics in 2008, they were forced to dispatch 33,000 exterminators to keep the infestation from reaching the host city during the games. In just that one swarm, the cicadas damaged and devoured over 3.2 million acres of agricultural land, and threatened to shut down the Olympic games altogether.

Biblical accounts of actual locust swarms may seem like lore but are as real as any swarm of cicadas that happen today. Yet locusts loomed even larger on the nations throughout biblical times because during that specific historical context, most nations relied on agrarian means for sustenance, trade, and growth. When a locust swarm ravaged through cities and regions—mayhem, starvation, and death morosely ensued.

WHEN THE FIELDS MOURN

In the opening chapter of Joel, God describes the impact of these locusts when He speaks to the prophet: "For a nation has invaded my land, mighty and without number; its teeth are the teeth of a lion, and it has the fangs of a lioness. It has made my vine a waste and my fig tree splinters. It has stripped them bare and cast them away; their branches have become white" (v. 6–7).

Earlier in Joel 1 we discover that the emergence God referenced wasn't a normal one when one brood, or kind, of locust appears during a cycle. Rather, this invasion contained several different types of locusts converging on the land together. Scientists say that such a convergence typically happens only once every several hundred years, and usually only contain two types of broods at one time. Yet, from the record we read in the first chapter of Joel, we can see that when God sent the locusts, He sent all of them—the "gnawing," "swarming," "creeping," and "stripping" (v. 4). He called them all up from under the ground to do His bidding. What one group of locusts didn't destroy, the next group did. And what that group didn't ravage, the next group did.

Thus, when we read God's Word to the prophet Joel telling him to ask the people, "Has anything like this happened in your days or in your fathers' days?" (v. 2), the answer is no.

They had witnessed swarms of locusts during their days, sure. But they had never had swarms of swarms, all swarming at the same time.

That's why Joel is instructed to inform the people, "Tell your sons about it, and let your sons tell their sons, and their sons the next generation" (v. 3). God wanted everyone to remember this moment when the fields mourned and the land groaned from devastation.

GOD'S GREAT ARMY

Looking closely at the Scripture, we see that the locust invasion was not merely a natural phenomenon, but rather it was sent by God to make a spiritual point. As we observe in Joel 2, these swarms of locusts—along with other things—were caused by God Himself. They were, "My great army which I sent among you" (v. 25).

Yet even though the devastation was brought on by God to send a message, unfortunately many people just didn't get it—or maybe it ended up in their spam box of sorts. So God sent a mouthpiece—the prophet Joel—to fill them in on the situation.

What happened back then is often mirrored by what happens still today, and that is that the people of God far too often fail to recognize that what appears to be a natural phenomenon really is the supernatural work of God.

Turn on the evening news or political talk shows at any given time and you will be privy to turmoil and ruin on myriads of levels. If I wrote right now about the major stories currently claiming the headlines, this paragraph would soon be outdated. Give our nation a week or two, and we will see a whole new onslaught of distresses and issues before us. True, some stories rise to the surface as having a greater and more long-term impact, but the sheer volume of crisis in our land today is alarming.

Yet, despite it all, we rarely make a spiritual connection to any of it. We just think that the housing mortgage industry failed, the economy tanked, the collective health of our citizenry has diminished, families simply got redefined, prisons somehow became too full while government likewise grew too large.

We turn our heads to ignore the alarming costs of what insurance companies call "acts of God." We assume that it's just a storm here or a disaster there, ignoring the sound of the felling of the trees for the printing of the paper for that ever-growing receipt. From 1980 through

2013, we've had 170 such "acts of God"—weather or climate devastations that have each cost $1 billion or more. The National Climate and Data Center reports the combined cost of these disasters has exceeded one trillion dollars.[3] No typo there; that's a T for trillion, as in "tragic." Whether it is God manifesting Himself meteorologically or just a natural pattern of His earth's weather movements, we cannot discount the impact we have felt as a nation under crisis.

Some would argue that we live in the church age wherein Jesus Christ has taken the punishment for our sins and so we no longer face God's wrath, the locusts, or intentional weather disruptions. But in the book of Romans, we clearly discover that the root cause of destruction and devastation is often tied to the natural consequences of turning away from God. Time and time again in the first chapter of Romans, we read these words, "God gave them over . . ."

As a result of hearts hardening toward and turning from Him, God allowed—as the natural consequence of spiritual rebellion—internal damage and deterioration to occur, ultimately exhibiting itself in external ramifications affecting others as well. It's not that the people referenced in Romans didn't know God either. In fact we read, "For even though they knew God, they did not honor Him as God or give thanks" (v. 21). They had distanced themselves from God and His Word. This distance is the same distance we see in the Old Testament times of spiritual judgment that serves as the core cause of those judgments.

Individual, family, and societal mess still stems from the same cause—distance from God.

So while the methods may not line up identically between the Old Covenant era and the New, the root of individual, family, and societal mess still stems from the same cause—distance from God.

In our solar system, we had nine planets. I say "had" because Pluto has since been demoted from the term *planet* to the much lesser known term of being a Kuiper Belt object. But when I grew up, Pluto was a planet, so Pluto stays in my illustration. It is the farthest known planet—or once-called "planet"—in our solar system. You could go to Pluto any time of the year, and you would be certain to freeze to death. Freezing temperatures dominate twenty-four hours a day and seven days a week. The reason Pluto is cold is because it is situated far, far away. Its distance from the sun keeps it cold.

On the other hand, Mercury is piping hot. As the closest planet to the sun, it is hot all the time. The reason Mercury is so hot is because it stays close to the sun. Mercury never leaves close proximity to the source of its heat. So if you tried to take a day trip to Mercury, you would burn up before you even got in the vicinity simply because it is too hot.

Now, both Mercury and Pluto are in our solar system. They are just not positioned the same in that system. They do not share the same proximity to the center of the system, the sun.

As believers in Christ, we are all in the same system. Yet some of us are Pluto Christians, and others are Mercury Christians. Some are cold all of the time. Depressed all of the time. Discouraged all of the time. Defeated all of the time. Yet others are more like Mercury—hot all of the time. Victorious. Joyous. Overcomers.

However, those are the two extremes. If we were to summarize the majority of the people who comprise the collective body of believers in our nation today, we would probably lean more toward a comparison with Earth than either Pluto or Mercury. This is because "Earth" saints are seasonal. On Sunday, it might be summertime. But on Monday, the winds of winter have already set in. Why? Because situations and circumstances have rotated believers into a seasonal pattern. And we all know what happens when hot weather and cold weather collide—chaos. Which is evident not only in so many believers' lives today, but also in the subsequent resultant outgrowth in our land.

DISTANT FROM GOD

The problem with our country today is not that God is not near. The problem is that we, the people, turn too quickly between near and far. We turn too quickly between God and other things that we look to in His place. As a result, America is undergoing the consequences, whether through active or passive wrath, because of distance from God.

Our nation's ills are not merely the result of corrupt politicians, terrorists, or extremists. Our troubles can be traced directly to ineffective Christians. The tragedy today is not that sinners sin; that's what they're expected to do, since mankind is born in sin and shaped in iniquity (Psalm 51:5; Ephesians 2:1–3). The real tragedy is that the church as a whole has failed to advance God's kingdom and principles in society in order to be a positive influence for good in our nation and in our world.

As we see in the passages from Joel, God sent His army of destruction to wake up *His people,* not to judge the rest of the world. God was Israel's problem Himself. God opened the doors for the locusts. God allowed the storms. And God gave them over to their enemies. God was the aggressor—not the Hittites, Philistines, or any other "ites" or "ines."

Just God.

And when God is your problem, only God is your solution.

The impetus behind the problems, even crises, occurring in our nation today is spiritual, even though the symptoms reveal themselves as physical, social, financial, racial, and more. Those are merely the fruit. That's why we'll never see lasting solutions until we—the body of believers—appropriately return to God. Until we hear His voice. Until we humbly fast and pray. Until we all get on the same page together of seeking His face.

Our solutions to our nation's problems will not first and foremost be found in the White House. Our solutions will first and foremost be found in God's house, because He is ultimately in charge and His people have priority access to Him.

Now is the time to invoke those solutions by calling on the spiritual leaders and believers in our land to initiate a national solemn assembly. Now is the time to clearly comprehend that God won't restore our nation until He first restores His church.

To turn our nation to God, we must, as His body, return to Him.

And we must do this after the example of a fourteen-year-old girl named Flo—with *all* our hearts.

2

Returning With All Your Heart

irst Samuel 7 recounts a story that rises out of the ashes of great pain. Set against the backdrop of anarchy and sorrow, we read in Judges that every man and woman "did what was right in [their] own eyes" (17:6; 21:25). Everyone had their own ideas. Each person lived by their own truths. This atmosphere created an up-and-down sort of existence.

At one point, the ark of the covenant—which represented the presence of God—had been captured and taken away at a price tag of over 30,000 Israelite men slaughtered in battle, along with the loss of several priests, not to mention the nation's pride.

The Philistines had stolen the ark and its mercy seat, which had faithfully served as the funnel for the Israelites' forgiveness. Yet in the presence of this new trophy, the Philistines found no mercy at all. Rather, they suffered greatly because of the ark. Their false god Dagon's statue fell face down before the ark repeatedly. Also, a deadly plague— similar to the bubonic—not only followed the ark from Philistine town to town, but also increased in severity as they sought to move the ark away from those who were dying (1 Samuel 5:1–6).

Eventually after several months, the Philistines wanted rid of this thing that represented the presence of God. So they sent it back to Israel. Back to where it belonged.

Yet even before the ark had left Israel, the people were largely without word from God: "Word from the LORD was rare in those days, visions were infrequent" (3:1). God wasn't doing much talking to His people at that time. This is because a breach had occurred—a chasm in their relationship due to their constant dismissal of Him.

As the Israelites began to feel the weight of their actions more frequently, they began to complain to God about all that had been happening to them—the oppression by their enemies, the economic hardships, and more. And though the ark was returned, the people of Israel still suffered at the hands of the Philistines. Apparently, their "truths" hadn't positioned them as a nation very well after all.

THE CALL FOR ALL

When they cried out to God, the prophet Samuel told them what to do. "If you return to the Lord with all your heart, remove the foreign gods and the Ashtaroth from among you and direct your hearts to the LORD and serve Him alone; . . . He will deliver you from the hand of the Philistines" (v. 3). In this, Samuel gave the Israelites a formula for the freedom, victory, and stability they so desired as a nation, and that formula is summarized in one word: *All.*

He told them to "return to the Lord with *all* your heart."

All. It was as simple, and as difficult, as that.

As creator of the universe, God didn't care to share His glory with impotent deities and Ashtaroth idols. None of those things was there when He parted the Red Sea so that the Israelites could escape the Egyptian army. None of those wooden carvings had brought water from a rock in the wilderness. None of the Ashtaroth infused the air with oxygen or caused the rain to wet the earth. Not one of the stones or statues knew the names of those who looked to them as idols, let alone every hair on their heads. God knew everything.

When it came to sharing glory with inanimate objects made from the very hands God Himself had given to humans, He would share none of it. Because God not only wanted, but also required, it all.

All.

It's one word, yet it impacts everything.

What if the sun only partially held the Earth in its gravitational orbit?

What if an airplane only partially filled its interior with oxygen for passengers to breathe?

What if our stomachs only partially digested the food that we put inside of it?

Or what if our skin only partially held our organs while veins only partially held our blood?

None of those "partials" would work out

He demands *all* of our hearts, all of us.

that well, as I'm sure you can imagine. Neither does giving God partial honor, partial positioning, and partial love in our lives. Partial doesn't cut it for God. He demands *all* of our hearts, all of us.

What's more, He won't shy away from sending judgments upon His people today as He did in the Old Testament times, or from allowing the natural consequences of removing Him from the equation as He does in the church age, in order to remind us what He ought to have—which is *all.*

The Israelites had not lived with an All-mentality. They had lived with an *And*-mentality. Yes, they had their temple, priests, and practices. In their minds, they had God. But it was always God-*and* something else.

God *and* human opinion.

God *and* manmade idols.

God *and* selfish mindsets.

God *and* superstition.

God *and* personal power.

God *and* gratification.

God *and* comfort.

God *and* success.

Sounds like America, doesn't it? We may not have our stones and statues, but we are a nation of idols. We are a nation of designer idols at that—fashionable ones. They may not be trees, beads, or rocks, but they are "idols" and "ands."

As a result, we are also a nation suffering underneath the atmospheric chaos of distance from God.

AMERICAN IDOLS

What is an American idol? First, let's look at what is an idol. An idol is any unauthorized source—person, place, thought, or thing—that you go to in order to meet a need. It is anything that eclipses God's rightful place in your life. An idol can also be a legitimate source God has provided to meet a need that you take further than you ought. You don't have to bow before a tree to have an idol. You don't have to kneel before a rock to have another god. All you have to do is go to something that God has not authorized as the source to meet your need, or take a source further than you should to meet it. When you do that, you have just bowed to another god.

Once you have brought another god into the equation, you have limited the true God's involvement in your life. God will not stoop to join other things that you look to in addressing needs in your life. God has a no-compete clause in His covenant. As 1 Samuel told the people, "Direct your hearts to the LORD and serve Him *alone*" (1 Samuel 7:3, italics added).

The reason why we are not witnessing the presence, power, and voice of God in our nation today is because many believers worship Him on Sunday morning, then invite other gods into the equation by Sunday afternoon.

America's idols come in all shapes and sizes. Even food can be an idol. Of course, food was given to us for good—to meet our needs for nourishment and health. Yet a large portion of us look to food to meet something other than what it was designed to do. Thus the terms "comfort food" and "diet" have entered the American vocabulary. Part of the current overtaxation of what is quickly becoming an anemic healthcare system stems from an improper use of food.

Satan tries to lure us by twisting a legitimate need into an illegitimate sin.

What Satan tries to do in luring us under idols of all sorts is twist a legitimate need into an illegitimate sin. For example, desire for food is good; gluttony is sin. Desire for sleep is good; laziness is sin. Desire for sex is good; immorality is sin.

Satan's strategy in setting up American idols is to play on legitimate God-given desires within us and turn them into something illegitimate. He knows that desire cannot be avoided or ignored—we have legitimate needs planted within us. So what Satan attempts to do is to warp those needs and desires by influencing how we seek to meet them.

Do we look to God's precepts and principles as our guiding force, or do we pull a "God-*and*" solution? Do we choose the world's ways of dealing with our personal debt or finances and then just sprinkle a little Jesus on top? Remember, the formula of "God-*and*" doesn't work. The formula that works is simple: All. He wants all our heart devoted to Him alone.

MORE AMERICAN IDOLS

America's idols come in other forms as well. Just to name a few to which we bow, there is materialism—buying more stuff than we would ever truly use. Then there is selfishness, which keeps our thoughts and actions ingrown rather than using our time, talents, and treasures for others' good and God's glory.

We can add the twin idols of sports and entertainment. Either (or both) becomes an idol when the activity goes further than meeting a need to enjoy life and begins to dominate our lives through our finances, schedules, or worship. When we place sports or entertainment figures, despite their lifestyles, on the pedestal of hero, they become another god in our minds.

When we embrace popular opinion and political correctness, causing us to hold our tongues rather than truly proclaiming God's truth, they have become an idol as well.

There is even the idol of religion. We have our checklists of do's and don'ts. We go through the motions. Perform our rituals. And then we pat ourselves on the back, all the while remaining distant from God.

Many idols are more subtle. There's the idol of accomplishment—also known as achievement, or you can call it personal success, where we seek to climb the ladder, while setting Christ's basin and towel aside. There is also the idol of politics—wrapping Christianity in the American flag. Or the idol of ethnicity—allowing our culture and race to dictate our values and choices more so than God.

And, again, while none of these idols is necessarily an idol at its root—it is when it begins to usurp God and His rightful place in our thoughts and actions. Each idol becomes competitive with God's plans, and it removes His hand of favor from our lives and from our land.

THE VOICE—THE RIGHT VOICE

A number of years ago, my son Anthony sang on the hit TV show *The Voice*. It was exciting watching him entertain people with his gift of singing. I also grew in my respect for him as I observed Anthony being a light to the lost in Hollywood during that time.

But there is another voice I want to talk about in this chapter—and that is the voice of God. It is the voice that the Israelites struggled to hear as recorded in Joel and also in 1 Samuel. It is also a voice we struggle to hear in our nation today.

But it is the one Voice we should be listening to the most.

When our country shook under the weight of terror on September 11, 2001, our Congress made a critical decision. They sought the voice of God. That evening, after two towers had fallen in New York and lives were lost there, in Washington, D.C., and in rural Pennsylvania, senators joined with representatives on the front steps of our nation's Capitol. Democrats stood next to Republicans as Congress convened at this unusual location on this unusual eve.

Following words of hope, victory, and justice—along with a moment of silence—with the eyes of nearly every American upon them as they were broadcast across all of the airwaves of our land, our Congress erupted into an impromptu prayer, even though they may not have known that they were praying. They may not have known they were praying because this prayer was couched in a song.

Most people don't realize that the song our Congress sang that night, "God Bless America," is indeed a prayer. We read this in its opening stanza, written in 1938 when war raged in Europe (a war America would soon enter). The stanza ends:

Let us all be grateful for a land so fair,
As we raise our voices in a solemn prayer.

And then came the chorus, "God bless America, land that I love ..."

A SOLEMN PRAYER, A SOLEMN ASSEMBLY

A solemn prayer. That's not too far from what God told His prophets to have His people do in times of crisis or distance from Him. He called it something a bit different, but not by much. He called it a solemn assembly, or a sacred gathering as we looked at in the last chapter. As we saw, if the Israelites wanted to fix the locust problem that they were facing, then they needed to hear the voice of the locust sender. They needed a solemn assembly to call on His name.

A solemn assembly was the means through which God brought about revival both in biblical times and later historical ones. In a number of the major occurrences of national revival recorded in the Old Testament, a solemn assembly, or a time of prayer and/or fasting, preceded the revival.[1] Multiple occurrences of these sacred gatherings happened elsewhere as well.[2] In the Old Testament period, the prescribed solemn assemblies included the Sabbath (Leviticus 23:3), the Feast of Passover and the Feast of Unleavened Bread (Leviticus 23:4–8), the Feast of Weeks (Numbers 23:28–26), the Feast of Trumpets (Leviticus 23:23–25), the Day of Atonement (Leviticus 23:26–32), and the Feast of Booths (first and eighth day, Leviticus 23:33–36).

In the New Testament period, the concept of the solemn assembly—or sacred gathering—is carried over as well. The church itself was birthed out of a multi-day prayer meeting that culminated in what is known as the Day of Pentecost, or Feast of Weeks.[3]

Likewise, every major revival in American history has begun through times of fasting and prayer coupled with a collective solemn assembly.

As noted earlier, in Israel the call to a solemn assembly was initiated by the civic leadership, priests, or the prophets. Sometimes these leaders worked alone, but often they worked in conjunction with each other. At the start, the call most often went to a small group of leaders who then brought it to the larger general body.

In the case we read about earlier in Joel, the prophet spoke on behalf of God directly to the people. The prophet said, "Rend your heart and not your garments . . . return to the Lord your God. . . . Blow a trumpet in Zion, consecrate a fast, proclaim a solemn assembly" (Joel 2:13, 15).

A solemn assembly was a sacred gathering calling God's people to renew their covenantal relationship with Him and to repent—namely a turning away from sin and a turning back to God. This, in turn, ushered in the rhythm of revival, resulting in the return of God's manifest presence among His own, and their land.

THE HEART OF THE MATTER

A solemn assembly only works if the people's hearts are in it. It doesn't work just because somebody puts it on the calendar, makes a web page, sets up a social media campaign, and people show up. In the passage we just looked at in Joel, God says to rend your heart and not your garments. In other words, this thing only works if it is internally driven and not merely externally enacted.

If we as a nation simply go through the formality of a solemn assembly without truly humbling our hearts before God and seeking Him first, then we will have wasted our time. Because the heart of the matter *is* the heart of the matter. A solemn assembly involves getting our hearts to beat in cadence with God's own. It's returning to Him so that He can return His favor, covering and protecting us.

When I go to the doctor for my annual exam and they check the flow of my blood throughout my body, they are measuring the strength of my heart. If my heart is not working, then nothing else is going to work either. Parts of our bodies will literally die when they don't get blood pumped to them. Blood is the source of life, and the heart disseminates that source.

Let Him be the center of our lives, communities, and nation. That is the only strategy for long-term, effective national reform.

When God says to return to Him with all of our hearts, He is saying to return to Him as our fundamental source. Let Him be the center of our lives, homes, churches, communities, and nation. He must flow through all that we do. That is the only strategy for long-term, effective national reform. His kingdom agenda must flow through every area of our lives, causing us to live all of life under God.

I've got a trash compacter in my home. I like the trash compacter because now that the kids are grown, taking out the trash is solely my job. So I'll run that smasher over and over again until you think it just couldn't smash anymore. And then I'll run it one more time. If you are familiar with a trash compacter, then you know the reason we put trash in there is to manage our trash—not to get rid of it. That's because eventually, no matter how well it smashes the trash, it will fill up.

When it fills up, I have to take the trash to the curb for the pick-up.

Unfortunately today, much—if not most—of what we do in our nation to try and solve political, racial, economic, social, and all sorts of ills, trash, and mess, is try to manage it. We stuff it down. Stomp on it. Smash it. Throw money at it. Or pretend it doesn't exist. All the while, God is giving us an open invitation to get rid of it altogether.

Return to Me, He says, and I'll pick it up.

Bring it to me, He calls, and I'll take care of it.

Come to Me, He gestures; I've got this.

Friends, we come by turning our hearts toward Him.

I've lived in my home for over four decades, and not once has the trashman rung my doorbell and asked to pick up my trash. I have to go to him. Likewise, God has asked us to take the mess of our nation to Him. He's waiting for us to move toward Him. So many of us are standing around looking at the plight of our nation and shaking our heads, asking, "When is God going to do something?" We are waiting on God to act. Yet, all the while, God is shaking His head as He waits on us. His Word has already given us the next steps—the blueprint—for what we need to do to get our nation turned around and on track.

NOW IS THE TIME

As Christians, we hold the destiny of our great land in our hands and in our hearts. God has not hidden His solution step. He has not kept silent. With all of the decay and destruction that we face on so many levels in our country, isn't now the time to come together and seek Him collectively? Isn't now the time to call for a solemn assembly?

Second Chronicles 15 provides a perfect illustration, reminding us where our nation is right now as well as how important it is that we quickly make changes—head back to God before we witness any more destruction. We read,

> For many days Israel was without the true God and without a teaching priest and without law . . . In those times there was no peace to him who went out or to him who came in, for many disturbances afflicted all the inhabitants of the lands. Nation was crushed by nation, and city by city, for God troubled them with every kind of distress. (vv. 3, 5–6)

What was wrong? Three crucial things were missing in Israel's national life. The same three things are missing in America as well. Briefly, the first missing item was "the true God."

The chronicler was not saying that the Israelites had become atheists or no longer believed in God. He wasn't saying that attendance at the temple was down. The sacrificial fires at the temple were still burning. But Israel had lost a correct view of God, and the nation was no longer accomplishing His agenda.

The Israelites wanted a convenient God, one they could control. Essentially, they wanted a kingdom without a King. They wanted a figurehead, a puppet with strings. Yet if you have a God you can control, then you're god instead of Him. Any god, or king, you can boss around isn't the true God, or King.

The true God does not adjust to you. You adjust to Him.

The Israelites didn't want the true God interfering with their national life, reminding them that He had an agenda greater than their personal interests and desires. Our nation doesn't want a God like that either. Our nation wants to pay homage only—to offer a nice little prayer before public meetings while simultaneously leaving God's perspective out of the details.

> **Once God is removed from or marginalized in a culture, . . . God becomes one's fiercest enemy and worst nightmare.**

The second thing missing in Israel was a lack of teaching priests. Again, the text doesn't say there were no priests. But the priests had stopped teaching the truth. They had traded enlightenment for entertainment. Worship had degenerated into a social club. The church was no longer the center of life and conscience in the culture, calling people to take God seriously. Israel was suffering from an absence of spiritual leaders who honored the authority of Scripture.

Too often today in America, we find this very same thing. Too many pastors preach to please. They fear that someone might say, "Well, I didn't like that sermon," and leave the church. But if the pastor preached God's Word, then that's the wrong response. The issue is whether the message is true, not whether it is popular. Politicians need to be popular. Preachers need to tell the truth.

The third missing ingredient in Israel was God's law. When a culture has a false view of God built on bad information, God begins to remove the restraint of His law, and evil grows unbridled. What you and I are witnessing today in the rapid deterioration of our nation is the reality that God is removing more of His restraint.

Once God is removed from or marginalized in a culture, then the righteous standard for a society is gone and God becomes one's fiercest enemy and worst nightmare, as we experience the natural consequences of distancing ourselves from Him (Romans 1:18–31). That's what had happened in Israel. And that's what is happening on a number of levels today in our land.

When the rule of God's truth goes missing, chaos replaces community. You cannot have order and structure in society without God.

The stunning thing about the situation in Second Chronicles 15 is that it is similar to what we've been looking at in Joel and 1 Samuel as well. It is what shows up as a pattern in the other solemn assemblies throughout Scripture.[4] That is that God was the cause of Israel's distress, not the sinners in the culture, and not even Satan.

If God is dismissed, it doesn't matter whom we elect or what programs we initiate. Until we reconnect with Him, we won't be able to fix what's wrong or spend enough money to bail our way out of our dilemmas.

The more we sideline God, the worse things will become.

This is the heart of our problem in America today. Too many individuals, families, churches, and communities want to keep God on the fringes of the decisions that are made. He can be accessible if we have a need, but we can keep Him far enough away from the center so that He doesn't start messing with our plans and pleasures.

As long as we keep God at a distance, He will not take over the control panel of our land, and unrighteousness will continue to rule. He will be close enough for invocations and benedictions but not part of the decisions in between.

Yet as the people of Israel set God on the outskirts, the outcome was destruction and demise. We read, "There was no peace to him who went out or to him who came in, for many disturbances afflicted all the inhabitants" (v. 5). That sounds like a high crime rate. "Nation was crushed by nation, and city by city" (v. 6a). That is a picture of conflict on both the local and the international levels.

And in verse 6 we once again see the cause: "For God troubled them with every kind of distress." In other words, God identified Himself as the responsible party—"God troubled them."

The more we sideline God, the worse things will become (Romans 1:18–31), as He releases us to the natural, negative consequences of abandoning Him. God isn't interested in being an addendum; He demands and deserves our all.

If we want to experience restoration in our country, we—as His body—will have to give Him all.

3

The Unshakeable Kingdom

On your smartphone, tablet, or even perhaps by the side of your bed, you have an alarm clock. Alarm clocks have a major assignment: letting us know that it's time to wake up. They have been preset to go off in the morning with a ringtone, song, or radio station in order to let people know they should no longer be sleeping. It's time to wake up.

Have you ever noticed that your alarm sometimes goes off at the most inconvenient time? Maybe you're in the middle of a dream you aren't ready to end, or you are sleeping soundly. Whatever the case, your alarm jolts you into reality in such a way that you may choose to resist it rather than respond. By resisting it, you hit the snooze button. That buys you ten more minutes of slumber.

Yet in what feels like it must be much less than ten minutes, your alarm goes off again, letting you know that the comfort of the covers must be set aside. It is time to start your day. Because whether you like it or not, responding to the alarm clock is critical if you want to accomplish much of anything at all.

God had alarm clocks in the Bible; they were individuals. We call them prophets. Prophets were God's alarm clocks sent by Him to wake up His people. The prophets sounded the alarm in order to call His people to a spiritual response. These prophets would speak on God's behalf in order to stir His own out of their stupor.

In the same way that our alarm clocks today aren't always appreciated when they interrupt our rest and relaxation, biblical prophets weren't always appreciated either when they sounded the divine alarm. They weren't always received well when they sought to wake the people up from their cozy situation.

Yet sometimes the situation the prophet was sent into wasn't so cozy and still at all. It would be more akin to a nightmare that had gone on way too long. A rumbling had set in among the prophet's people, causing shaking to occur in all that was once peaceful. Similar to the tremors during an earthquake, the normal functioning routine of society rattled, broke, and brought destruction. Such was the case for the prophet Haggai when he was asked to speak to the nation during a time of great shaking and alarm.

HAGGAI'S ALARM CLOCK

The Bible is divided into sections called Major Prophets and Minor Prophets. The Major Prophets contain the longer books such as Ezekiel and Isaiah while the Minor Prophets contain the smaller books, like Haggai which has only two chapters. Yet while Haggai might be considered a Minor Prophet, he voiced a major message. His alarm was necessarily loud and urgent.

Haggai sounded his message after a period of seventy years in which Israel felt the wrath of God in Babylon. The people had rejected the earlier prophets, like Jeremiah, thus opening the door for the Babylonian invasion, destruction of their temple, and enslavement of their people for nearly a century. During these days, most of them lived miserably in a foreign land, desperate to come out of captivity.

Haggai declared his message to the returning Jews who now made their way back to Israel from Babylon. In fact, most of them have been back in Israel for fifteen years when Haggai proclaimed his message. By this time, the temple should have been rebuilt. God had provided all that they needed in order to do that—the wood, resources, and protection. But the problem that Haggai addresses from the start is that the temple still sits undone.

Now before you think that this is a prophet upset about a building plan gone awry, we need to look even deeper at the cultural and spiritual context, which we find in the books of Ezra and Zechariah. In Ezra, we read that the reason for the temple's lack of completion isn't due to a lack of supplies. Rather, it is due to the opposition the Israelites faced in its rebuilding. It was a hassle. It became difficult. They faced resistance from their enemies, which led to discouragement. In the end, they just decided it was far easier to put that project on hold.

In the Old Testament culture, the temple was not the local community center. Rather, the temple was the location of the manifest presence of God. Here God's glory dwelled in the midst of His people. So when the people of Israel said they did not have the time, energy, or strength to rebuild the ruins of God's temple, they weren't merely talking about a building. They were talking about not having the priority to pursue God's presence in their midst. They were satisfied with God in the vicinity, much like many of us are today. Yet

The lack of repairing the temple was an indicator light of the Israelites' distance from God.

there is a big difference between God on the loop of life and God in the midst of it.

We see this verified through another prophet, Zechariah, whom God sent to prophesy to the same group of people at the exact same time. We read, "The Lord was very angry with your fathers. Therefore say to them, 'Thus says the Lord of hosts, "Return to Me," declares the Lord of hosts, "that I may return to you," says the Lord of hosts. "Do not be like your fathers'" (1:2–4).

When we put the two prophets' messages together, we read of Zechariah calling for a return to God while Haggai is calling for a concrete manifestation of this return through the building of the temple. The messages don't contradict each other. Instead, they go hand in hand. The lack of repairing the temple was simply an indicator light of the Israelites' distance from God—similar to the indicator lights that come on in your vehicle to let you know that something deeper is wrong.

There had been a return to the land. But there had not been a return to God. They had put the old ways and location of Babylon behind them but they had not turned toward God and His ways. As a result, God disrupted the normalcy of life for the Israelites by calling for a drought—both in rain and in the production by the people (Haggai 1:10–11). This shaky situation led to economic instability, governmental instability, relational instability, personal instability, and more. All because the people had returned to the land but they had not returned to God. They had not truly repented.

> **The purpose of repentance is to reestablish fellowship with God, reconciliation with others, and also . . . limit the consequences of the sin.**

Let's recall what repentance truly is: Repentance involves not only being sorry, but also a "change of mind" about the offense—seeing the offense as God sees it. This then will prompt a turning away from the wrong behavior and toward the right behavior. It also will cause us to bring an offering of restitution if at all possible or needed. The purpose of repentance is not only to reestablish fellowship with God and reconciliation with others but also to cancel, reverse, or limit the consequences of the infraction or the sin.

The problem many people in our nation miss when it comes to repentance is that they may turn away from something yet not always turn to God. This is a critical element. We can turn from a certain sin yet still remain as miserable as before because we have not turned to God. It's like driving the wrong way on the interstate highway and choosing to take the exit ramp. We no longer are traveling the wrong way, but we take the overpass and turn back on the road going the opposite direction, thinking we have corrected our problem.

A LESSON FROM THE PRODIGAL SON

Most of us know the story of the prodigal son (Luke 15:11–32). The wayward son blew his inheritance and ended up lying wasted in a pigpen, eating the scraps that he could find. If he would have merely cleaned himself up and left the pigpen, he would not have completed the cycle of a return, nor would he have gotten anything that he needed to live out his days well. Only when he returned to his father did he receive the benefits of the relationship with his father.

It's not enough to have people turn from behaviors that do not glorify or honor God. It's not even enough to have people turn to church and fill our buildings to the brim. Until there is a returning to God to be the followers Christ died to procure in our land, we will not be partakers of the benefits of an intimate relationship with Him. We need God's manifest presence in our lives, not merely His name on a nice plaque on our walls.

A PROBLEM OF PRIORITIES

In the book of Haggai we discover a common reason that many do not return to God. "Then the word of the Lord came by Haggai the prophet, saying, 'Is it time for you yourselves to dwell in your paneled houses while this house lies desolate?'" (Haggai 1:3–4). God was telling the people that they did not make time to rebuild His house yet had plenty of time to build their own houses. In fact, God pointed out that they had time to panel their houses—using the materials He had supplied for the temple.

Essentially, He is telling them that the problem at hand is not a time nor a resource problem. They had more than enough time and resources to construct, build, decorate, and restore their own homes. The problem at hand, rather, was that they didn't have time for God.

The problem was one of priority.

We all know that we will make time for what is a priority. Whether it's a hobby, a sporting event, shopping, movies, or conversations with friends—we will find the time. But when it comes to prayer, meditating, or seeking God's presence, we will often join the Israelites in Haggai's day and simply say, "It's not time for that right now. I'll get to that later." All the while our families, churches, schools, communities, and nation are going into disarray. But we look good. We laugh well. We eat right. We live in nice homes. We drive nice cars. Our pets are groomed on time. Our shows are watched on time.

Friends, time was not the Israelites' problem, and neither is it ours today.

MONEY AND TIME

The message to the church at Ephesus in the book of Revelation is the message to the Israelites in Haggai's day and the message to the church of America in our day: "I have this against you, that you have left your first love" (Revelation 2:4).

It's not that we in America haven't produced scholars from our seminaries and Bible schools. Nor is it that we haven't built enormous campuses and churches where people can meet once or twice a week. It's not that we haven't created Christian schools or sung Christian songs or published Bibles in every color, shape, and for every nuance of life. No, I don't think God would say that we haven't done any of those things. We have, and more.

But something tells me He would say that we have left our first love—Him. Because if you want to measure someone's heart, you look at two things—their money and their time. The average evangelical Christian gives 3.7 percent of what they earn back to God.[1] That means the average evangelical Christian is robbing God 6.3 percent of what He gives them, at a minimum. The 10 percent tithe is a minimum number. Yet our houses are getting bigger, our cars are getting newer, our clothes are getting finer, but the message of God's Word to a nation and a world in need continues to be truncated in its reach.

God has more than enough in His storehouse to impact our nation for good, but why would He want to give to His people who are only stealing from Him? And while you might think that thievery is a harsh word to use, it is the word God used in Malachi where we read, "Will a man rob God? Yet you are robbing Me! But you say, 'How have we robbed You?' In tithes and offerings" (3:8).

Because the Israelites of Haggai and Zechariah's day valued their own leisure and their own pleasure greater than God's manifest presence, they used both their money (resources) and time on themselves, similar to us today. As a result, they suffered loss. Listen carefully to what God said through Haggai:

Now therefore, thus says the Lord of hosts, "Consider your ways! You have sown much, but harvest little; you eat, but there is not enough to be satisfied; you drink, but there is not enough to become drunk; you put on clothing, but no one is warm enough; and he who earns, earns wages to put into a purse with holes."

Thus says the Lord of hosts, "Consider your ways! Go up to the mountains, bring wood and rebuild the temple, that I may be pleased with it and be glorified," says the Lord. "You look for much, but behold, it comes to little; when you bring it home, I blow it away. Why?" declares the Lord of hosts, "Because of My house which lies desolate, while each of you runs to his own house. Therefore, because of you the sky has withheld its dew and the earth has withheld its produce. I called for a drought on the land, on the mountains, on the grain, on the new wine, on the oil, on what the ground produces, on men, on cattle, and on all the labor of your hands." (Haggai 1:5–11)

Essentially, God not only cut a hole in their pockets; He cut a hole in His own provisions to them, even the fruitfulness of the labor of their hands. They bought more, built more, wanted more . . . but ended up with less. Nothing satisfied them.

Consider your ways, God says. Return to Me.

God had already provided the wood and materials for the Israelites to restore His temple (Ezra 3:7). But as we saw earlier, they had used it to remodel or make their own homes. Now they were told to go up into the mountains and cut down the wood themselves since they had taken the goodness of God and used it on their own wants rather than on His plan and the manifestation of His glory.

Yet what they didn't realize, or what they had forgotten, is that God can curse as easily as He can bless. He can withhold as easily as He can provide. And He will do just that to remind His own of His rightful position in our lives.

> **How do we get back to where God is in a rightful position? By loving Jesus Christ with all of our hearts.**

How do we get back to that place where God is in a rightful position? By loving Jesus Christ with all of our hearts. It comes down to that single-syllable word again: All. Whatever you love, with all of your heart, will be your priority. You won't have to force it, schedule it, or set up a reminder on your smartphone to do it. Has anyone ever had to remind a young man who is in love to call the one whom he loves? No, he just does it.

Likewise, when we—as the body of Christ—return to loving Jesus Christ, with all of our hearts, we will return to God. We will want to see His temple—His presence and glory—manifest in our midst. We will make our decisions based on what best advances His kingdom. We will give accordingly, pray accordingly, love others accordingly, and live accordingly. Not because we're tied to a list of do's and don'ts, but because what you love transforms how you live.

It is time for each of us to truly love Jesus Christ—with all of our hearts.

When we do, we will see our nation restored—as the Israelites did.

THE ISRAELITES RESPONDED

In Haggai 1:12, we see that the people responded rightly to God when He declared their distance from Him through His prophet. We read, "Then Zerubbabel the son of Shealtiel, and Joshua the son of Jehozadak, the high priest, with all the remnant of the people, obeyed the voice of the Lord their God and the words of Haggai the prophet, as the Lord their God had sent him. *And the people showed reverence for the Lord*" (italics added),

The people listened to the prophet and turned toward God. They showed Him reverence by once again making Him their highest priority. In response to their reverence, God revealed to them the next portion of His plan for them. He spoke of a shaking that was about to take place. "'As for the promise which I made you when you came out of Egypt, My Spirit is abiding in your midst; do not fear!' For thus says the LORD of hosts, 'Once more in a little while, I am going to shake the heavens and the earth, the sea also and the dry land. I will shake all the nations'" (Haggai 2:5–7a).

God begins by giving His people assurance. He recognizes the uncertainties that they have been facing, the fear in which they have been living, and the shaking that they have experienced already due to the drought He called not only on their land but also on their labor (Haggai 1:10–11). So He tells them not to be afraid.

A WHOLE LOT OF SHAKING GOING ON

After assuring them that they have nothing to fear, He tells them that they can expect some shaking: "I am going to shake the heavens and the earth."

God says that He is going to once more shake things up. But this time will do so in order to turn things around. The method is the same—it's a disruption in the normalcy of life. But the objective this time is something different altogether.

God tells His people He will involve Himself in a graphic and visible way in order to shift things around. But His end goal, this time, is unlike the end goal in chapter one of Haggai. We read, "'I am going to shake the heavens and the earth, the sea also and the dry land. I will shake all the nations; and they will come with the wealth of all nations, and I will fill this house with glory,' says the Lord of hosts. 'The silver is Mine and the gold is Mine,' declares the Lord of hosts. 'The latter glory of this house will be greater than the former,' says the Lord of hosts." Then he declares, "'And in this place I will give peace'" (Haggai 2:. 6–9).

In summary, He says:

I will shake the nations.
They will bring their wealth.
I will fill this house with glory.
The latter glory will be greater than the former.
This place will know My peace.

This time, God is shaking things up in order to bring to the Israelites the gold, silver, and glory that belongs in His temple. He is taking the wealth of those who do not call on His name and giving it to those who do (Proverbs 13:22). Through this, He is also producing that one elusive life element so many of us crave but rarely experience—peace.

God will often lead His people through a shaky scenario prior to bringing to birth His plan for them, prior to bringing about something new. Remember when He led Israel out of Egypt? He put them in an uncomfortable situation. They faced Pharaoh on their left and the Red Sea on their right. But the reason God allowed this uncomfortable situation was because He was getting ready to do something entirely new. He was getting ready to do something they had never seen before. Opening up the Red Sea was a shake-up, an interruption of the normal flow of things. He was getting their attention.

God tells the Israelites that this new shaking is not to punish them or correct them, but to provide for them.

When God is getting ready to do something new in your own personal life and even in our families, communities, and our nation, He will regularly shake things up first. It can feel like a frightening and painful situation because we can't always see the new thing that is coming. But that is why God says, "Do not fear"—He is doing it on purpose. That is why He tells the Israelites that this new shaking is not to punish them or correct them, but rather to provide for them.

It is similar to when an expectant mother goes into labor. Those labor pains are how the baby gives notice that he or she wants out. Yet in serving this notice of an ultimately good event, the baby creates discomfort, anguish, even agony. It becomes a shaky situation. In this uncomfortable situation something new is breaking forth—someone growing and developing beneath the surface is getting ready to be delivered.

God will frequently allow labor pains to occur—whether it be in an individual, a relationship, an organization, or a nation—when He is getting ready to deliver something new. He creates a shaky situation that forces the person or people involved to deal with and recognize the new place He is taking them to, or the new situation He is bringing about. Otherwise, you may miss the birth, overlook the shift, and fail to benefit from the delivery.

God shakes things up to get our attention and to reveal the new reality He is creating. He also shakes things up to shake us loose from those who are holding onto us. What's more, He will often do this suddenly. But the danger is—in the swiftness and unexpectedness of the way God moves—it is easy to miss it.

GOD HAS SOMETHING TO SAY

Many of you grew up in homes like I did where an adult made you turn off the television when there was thunder and lightning outside. Now, the reason my grandma made us do that was because of a simple statement she would always say, "God is talking."

As a young boy, my question in response was, "Why does God have to talk during one of my favorite shows! Why can't He talk during Howdy Doody or something I don't like? Why does He have to mess up my day!"

My grandma's reply never wavered. "Turn it off, Tony—God has something to say."

Now, of course, back then I didn't care that God had something to say. I had something to watch. But therein was the problem, and therein is also a reflection of the greater problem evident today in the body of Christ. I had no sense that I needed to listen to heaven simply because God had created discontinuity on earth.

This is similar to what happens to most of us today, especially those of us who follow Christ. We haven't learned to pay attention yet. We haven't learned to listen, to turn off the televisions of our time—the tablets, phones, work, travel, hobbies, interests, entertainment, sports, spending, whatever—in order to sit still and listen.

Rather, we just get annoyed that the bailout didn't quite bail us out. Or that another hurricane, flood, fire, or tornado has destroyed yet another town or community. Or that we are in yet another international battle. Or that crime and delinquency have become such a regular way of life that they are affecting our cities and our lifestyles, making normal activities like eating out, attending a movie, or going to the mall a real risk. Or that fatherhood somehow went missing. Our schools graduate fewer qualified young adults. Our churches have lost both influence and impact as their bells ring of formality and fashion rather than humility and devotion.

We haven't yet learned that when God disrupts the natural order of things in our lives and in our land, it's not just a bad day or week.

God has something to say.

God is shaking things up either to redirect our priorities back to Him (as we saw in Haggai 1) or to usher in new life through a new delivery by birthing a shift in our hearts, minds, and situations (as we saw in Haggai 2). Either way, He is awakening us to listen.

BUT THAT'S THE OLD TESTAMENT

Now, in case you are thinking that this is a great story and a great truth in the Old Testament with little value to our lives and country today, let's look at the New Testament and the current church age. In the book of Hebrews we read of this same shaking and its purposes. It says,

See to it that you do not refuse Him who is speaking. For if those did not escape when they refused him who warned them on earth, much less will we escape who turn away from Him who warns from heaven. And His voice shook the earth then, but now He has promised, saying, "YET ONCE MORE I WILL SHAKE NOT ONLY THE EARTH, BUT ALSO THE HEAVEN." This expression, "Yet once more," denotes the removing of those things which can be shaken, as of created things, so that those things which cannot be shaken may remain. Therefore, since we receive a kingdom which cannot be shaken, let us show gratitude, by which we may offer to God an acceptable service with reverence and awe; for our God is a consuming fire. (12:25–29)

God's strategy hasn't changed in the New Testament either. He is still shaking things up in order to turn lives around. He is shaking the visible in order to reveal the invisible—shaking what you can see in order for you to see what you could not previously see. This is similar to what happens when people dig for gold, particularly in areas of black sand. When the black sand is first brought in, you cannot see the gold—even though it is there. If someone were to try to pick through the sand to get to the gold, it would take years, if possible at all. So the gold diggers pour the sand mixed with gold onto a shaking table.

This shaking table then vibrates at such a rate and in such a direction and angle that it literally shakes the fine gold elements loose from the black sand and separates them so that they can then be harvested and used.

When you first look at the black sand on the table, before the table shaking begins, you won't see the gold. But after the shaking takes place, you will see the gold clearly glistening as it collects in an exit funnel.

Like the gold hidden in the sand, there is much going on in our lives and in our nation that we do not see. These are the things behind the scenes—in the heavenlies—where God is operating and Satan is combating and decisions are being made. Often it requires a shaking for us to recognize God's hand and movement in a situation.

The great tragedy in our material-based, logical nation is that events take place in our lives and in those of people around us in which we fail to make the spiritual connection. We have so divided the physical from the spiritual that we have lost access to recognizing, understanding, and using both the authority and the power of the kingdom.

All we see is uncertain economics, jobs being cut, relationships falling apart, churches closing their doors, sermons turning into fluff, and crime going up. We see all of that, yet we don't see that there is another kingdom—another Hand—shaking things behind the scenes. God is shaking things up to take us—the body of Christ—to a deeper experience with Him. To separate the sand from the gold, to open our eyes to His kingdom and His movement on earth.

When the richest nation in the world is unable to pay its bills, having to bail everyone out while simultaneously legislating immorality, with its prisons full to overflowing while its schools lose its students by droves ... and we just think its bad loans, we've missed it. If we just think it's bad politicians, we've missed it. If we just think it's a bad culture, we've missed it.

It is about God shaking things up and humbling us until we understand that He alone is God. It is about God trying to get our attention.

Have you ever been with a young child who desperately wants your attention but you are too distracted to give it? And that child starts shaking your leg, shaking your knees, jumping up and down, pulling on your arm ... doing anything and everything to get your attention. What do you eventually do? You give that child your attention.

Friends, God is trying to get our attention. He has something to say.

DO NOT FEAR

In the midst of the shaking all around us, we need to remember one thing. When God is bringing about a renewal—when we have deliberately and intentionally responded to His call like the people of Israel did by showing Him reverence—the shaking around us is not to be feared. Through it He is revealing His unshakeable kingdom. He is revealing what will last.

The greatest literal example of this is Rahab, the prostitute in Jericho. She hid the spies and aided in their escape. As they departed, the spies told Rahab to hang a scarlet rope from her window when the Israelites returned to invade Jericho and to stay within her home, along with her family. If they did, they would be safe (Joshua 2:16–21).

The Israelites then marched around the Jericho walls. The ground began to shake. The walls fell down. And Rahab, along with her family—in her home—was safe. While the world around her collapsed, as rocks shook and walls crumbled, Rahab's home was safe.

The interesting thing about this story is that Rahab's house was actually *on* the wall (v. 15). She wasn't in a safe zone. She wasn't out in a rural area. The spies didn't tell her to go hide in a shelter. Rather, Rahab was smack dab in the middle of the severest shaking going on. After all, the walls fell down. But Rahab, her home, and her family were kept safe. That little piece of the wall remained intact.

When God shakes things up to bring about renewal and an awakening, at first it might feel scary to us. It might seem like things are collapsing around us. But remember Rahab. Remember the wall. Remember Hebrews. Remember Haggai. Remember that God says do not fear when you have prioritized Him first.

Returning to God and making Him your top priority doesn't guarantee smooth sailing. As we have heard through the voice of the prophet Haggai, returning to God sometimes produces shaking. But when it does, if we will remain firmly committed to God's Word and what He has commanded us to do, like Rahab did, He will preserve us—as He goes about the process of shifting things around, shaking things loose and returning His goodness, gifts, and glory to His own.

4

The Return of the King

Every four years the eyes of America become riveted on the national election returns, as the people of America determine who will occupy the White House. People cast their votes because they want to influence who lives in that house. They want to choose who the first family of the United States will be.

There never is full agreement on this choice of the US president. Some vote for a Democrat, others for a Republican, and still others vote for an independent. Yet whatever the majority vote is at the end of the day will decide who is the next president.

That house at 1600 Pennsylvania Avenue in Washington, D.C., embodies much more than simply a residence for a family. Rather, it is a representative presence of leadership that affects the entire nation and, because of our international standing, the whole world.

Officially home to only one family, the White House has a lot to say about the millions of houses, businesses, and cities that comprise our nation. This one location wields enormous influence simply based on who lives there.

GOD'S HOUSE—THE TEMPLE

Friends, God also has a house. In the Old Testament, that house was called the temple. The temple existed as the representative residence of the presence of God among His people. When God chose to show His presence in history to humanity, He instructed them to construct Him a house. In fact, throughout Scripture, the temple is literally and frequently referred to as "God's house." Keep in mind, that doesn't mean He limited Himself to being there, but rather that was His specifically designated location for His experiential presence among His people. It is where His consecrated visage became manifest to those who came near.

The historical context of God's house began with the tabernacle, a roving tent through the wilderness. Yet when the Israelites reached the destination of their homeland, David's son Solomon built God a more formal house. All was well in this kingdom at the beginning as God's presence remained in His permanent house. Yet over time the people became more and more disinterested in the One who sat on high. And we discover that eventually God left His house.

Who knows how that leaving actually played out, but if we were to imagine it—it might have occurred this way. One day, after many similar days just like the one I am referring to now, God looked out over His kingdom of people and watched them go about their active ways. He recalled the vibrancy of their worship and the closeness of their hearts that had once existed and brought Him tremendous joy. Yet on this day—which was so similar to the many days

God packed up His experiential presence and left. When He did, Israel remained with a house yet no Lord.

before it—He looked out again and saw that no one even noticed Him anymore.

Conversations around the dinner table focused on each other, not on Him. People walked nearby but made no real effort to say hello. God heard laughter, saw the children running, smelled the meat cooking, and witnessed the businesses growing. Lives had become filled with busy agendas and self-serving interests. He was no longer needed, or so it seemed in their minds. He was no longer sought out, or even wanted. And so He sighed. It was a sigh, though, unlike the other sighs that had happened on the many similar days which had come before. Because this was a sigh of decision. After this sigh, God packed up His experiential presence and left. When He did, Israel remained with a house yet no Lord, a property yet no Person. A location yet no Love.

As a result, Israel immediately succumbed to loss. In fact, the book of Ezekiel focuses on this time when the people are now under discipline by God in Babylon. Due to their rebellion against Him and their idolatry, the Lord allowed them to be pulled away into places they did not want to go.

Their productivity slowed. In Babylon, they became trapped in an unending cycle of boredom where other people dictated their moves, decisions, and time. They had lost the freedom they had once enjoyed. Instead now their lives were stifled, their zeal gone, and their days, which had at one time been a robust experience, were now tiresome at best.

When God left His house because the people had left Him, the nation fell apart politically, socially, economically, spiritually, and relationally.

THE RETURN OF THE KING

Yet somewhere near Ezekiel 40, God's message through the prophet changed. God gave the prophet a vision of a new temple. The people of

God were now ready to respond to the heart of God, and so God would come back home. We read Ezekiel's words, "And the glory of the Lord came into the house by the way of the gate facing toward the east. And the Spirit lifted me up and brought me into the inner court; and behold, the glory of the Lord filled the house" (Ezekiel 43:4–5).

Israel would witness the return of the King.

WATER IN GOD'S HOUSE

If we flip forward a couple of chapters to Ezekiel 47, we read that the prophet is now being guided by the Lord's messenger, who is talking to him about, of all things, water. Why water?

In the Scriptures water is a sign of life, often intricately tied to the work of the Holy Spirit. In John 7, Jesus says that whoever believes in Him will have rivers of living water flowing out from within (v. 38). These rivers are a direct reference to the Spirit (v. 39). Just as water brings life to the physical body, the Spirit of God brings life to the spirit of man, and beyond.

So in Ezekiel 47, we discover this presence of water and life. Standing before the door of the house of God, Ezekiel sees water flowing from under the threshold toward the east. He also sees the water flowing down from the right side of the house, from south of the altar (v. 1).

After witnessing the presence and source of the water, we read Ezekiel's account: "He brought me out by way of the north gate and led me around on the outside to the outer gate by way of the gate that faces east. And behold, water was trickling from the south side" (v. 2). The water had begun to trickle outside of the perimeter of God's house into the surrounding areas.

Yet as the angel continued to lead Ezekiel, the water's trickle increased to a flow. What had started as a small area of water now reached as high as his ankles (v. 3), then his knees, his loins (v. 4), and eventually became so deep that he could have easily swum. "It was a river that I could not ford," Ezekiel wrote, "for the water had risen, enough water to swim in, a river that could not be forded" (v. 5).

At this point, the angel asked Ezekiel a rhetorical question, "Son of man, have you seen this?" Then he led the prophet to the bank of the river and explained the significance of what Ezekiel saw,

> These waters go out toward the eastern region and go down into the Arabah; then they go toward the sea, being made to flow into the sea, and the waters of the sea become fresh. It will come about that every living creature which swarms in every place where the river goes, will live. And there will be very many fish, for these waters go there and the others become fresh; so everything will live where the river goes. And it will come about that fishermen will stand beside it; from Engedi to Eneglaim there will be a place for the spreading of nets. Their fish will be according to their kinds, like the fish of the Great Sea, very many. But its swamps and marshes will not become fresh; they will be left for salt. By the river on its bank, on one side and on the other, will grow all kinds of trees for food. Their leaves will not wither and their fruit will not fail. They will bear every month *because their water flows from the sanctuary*, and their fruit will be for food and their leaves for healing." (vv. 8–12, italics added)

What had started in the house of God had now flowed throughout the land, bringing life to everything that it touched—even to that which had been dead. Flowing down into the Arabah and out toward the sea, the rivers of water would have hit what is called the Dead Sea. The Dead Sea, the lowest point on the earth, earned its name due to its high concentration of salt within it. The salt levels are so dense that the sea is unable to support life or growth in any capacity.

Yet even the Dead Sea came to life when the fresh waters overflowing from the sanctuary reached it. The angel spoke of the many fish and the resulting fishermen seeking them with their nets. Next to the fresh water would now also grow trees whose fruit would never fail and whose leaves would offer healing … all because the fresh life from God's house overflowed to the surrounding areas.

Keep in mind that the water didn't flow out of the sanctuary because the people of Israel created a "clean-water" program. The water brought life to the community, the Dead Sea, and everything surrounding it because God's presence was manifested in His house.

I've asked this question before and it is a question that still needs to be asked today: How can we—in America—have all of these churches with all these members led by all these preachers with all of these programs, money, and staff and yet still have all of this mess?

The answer to that question is simple and it has not changed: Because there is no water flowing out of God's house. We have missed the manifestation of His presence.

THE TEMPLE TODAY

God doesn't have a specific, single temple in the church age in which we now live, but Ephesians 2 tells us that the body of Christ is the temple of God (vv. 19–22). What the temple was in the Old Testament, the church is in the New Testament. Essentially, God now has a whole bunch of houses. And within those houses are those who have accepted Jesus Christ as their personal Savior and as a result, are now personal temples of God as well (1 Corinthians 3:16). So when these personal temples—you and I—gather together as a collective body, God's presence ought to be manifested to overflowing. Yet far too often, it is not.

For too many Christians, a two-hour church service is akin to going to a two-hour movie. During a movie, you sit in your seat—the lights are dimmed, the sound comes up, and for that length of time, you are entertained. You look to the screen to put on a show so that you can leave two hours later either speaking about how great it was or critiquing what was wrong. Movies are a spectator event. Unfortunately today church has become a similar thing. People attend to either check it off their list as a duty or to be entertained.

Another problem is when you go to the movies, no matter how good the actors are, you do not leave the theater having gotten to know the actors. The purpose of being in God's house is for you to experience and know *Him*, not simply to show up to see what can be done to make you feel better. God wants you to leave His house knowing Him more deeply than ever before, so that the abiding presence of His Spirit within you overflows and brings life to all that is around you.

THE CHURCH HOUSE OR THE WHITE HOUSE

When God returned His glory to the temple during Ezekiel's day, He wanted the people to experience His reality and for that reality to then overflow and change the culture around them. How things would work in society was determined by how things worked, or did not work, in the temple. If God had to leave the temple, the problems showed up in the streets. The same holds true today. Yet when God returned His manifest presence to the temple, the healing showed up in the streets as well.

What good is a beautiful church with great preaching if God isn't sought to bring victory through His manifest presence?

God's first concern during any political season is not the same as our first concern—it is not about what is happening, or going to happen, in the White House. God's first concern is what is happening, or not happening, in His house. If God can't get the church house right, it doesn't matter who we put in the White House. Judgment and healing start with the household of God. When we draw near to God so that His glory shows up as a regular occurrence in His house, it will overflow to the rest of society.

The issue we face today as the collective body of Christ is whether the glory of God is within us, within our midst, and within our churches. Yes, we have all of these nice new buildings packed full of people with nice new clothes being preached to by all of these eloquent and educated speakers. But is that our overarching agenda? It's not unlike a professional sports team. Pick your favorite team and ask this question: What good is a brand-new stadium with brand-new uniforms and brand-new coaches in front of a larger-than-ever crowd if the team only continues to lose?

Likewise, what good is a beautiful church with a wonderful choir, an awesome program, a remodeled facility, and great preaching if God isn't sought to bring victory to the lives of those in the sanctuary through His manifest presence? The purpose of the temple of God was for God's presence to be made real so that it would not only change the temple and those in it, but that it would then overflow into the culture.

Do you know the reason our culture is decaying and dying in so many ways? Because there is no water coming out of our temples—or, at best, it's a trickle. We have lost our flow.

Friends and fellow citizens, our problem today is not first and foremost the White House. Our problem is the church house. If God could ever get us straight in His house, He will overflow into our communities and our nation, bringing life where there was once only the stench of death. Yet how do we expect to get water flowing down the streets of our country if it can't even flow down the aisles of our churches?

Unfortunately, we've been so anesthetized by religion that we've been lulled to sleep by ritual. The goal of the kingdom-minded church is to so affect its members that they then affect the culture. It is to make God's Spirit felt, experienced, trusted, and known.

For example, when you see a fireplace, you see something that is contained in a specific location. Even so, the fireplace doesn't merely warm up the bricks. The fireplace warms up the entire room. God wants us to be so hot for Him that not only is His sanctuary on fire, but that the heat leaves the building and permeates the world around us. Our nation is not housed in our church buildings, and it never will be. But what is housed within us—God's Spirit—and within our churches ought to be so powerful, so authentic, and so life-giving that it touches every part of our land.

The question to us today is simple: Are we satisfied with a trickle? Or are we satisfied with ankle-deep of God? If that's all we want, then we need to stop complaining about our country. Because if we are not willing to be a part of the solution, then we have no right to say anything at all.

The solution to that which lies dead and dormant in our nation is within you. It's within me. It's within each of us who make up the body of Christ. When we collectively seek the return of God's manifest presence through hearts that are committed to and in love with Him, we will be the conduit through which God pours out His life-giving Spirit on our land.

PART 2

Returning
As the Church

5

"If My People"

In case I haven't made it clear yet, let me say it right here: The future of American culture is squarely in the hands of Christians.

Our problem is not so much the presence of unrighteousness as it is the loss of God's glory. Unrighteousness and evil have dominated our culture because God's glory has been marginalized, and that marginalization is primarily the result of the removal of Christ's lampstand from the church (Revelation 2:5). Make no mistake about it: America's future is not in the hands of the politicians or the social scientists. Most don't know what to do. They are "always learning and never able to come to the knowledge of the truth" (2 Timothy 3:7).

The reason the future of our culture is in the hands of Christians is that the cause of our cultural demise is spiritual. And if a problem is spiritual, its cure must be spiritual.

Based on the premise of this book, you might be saying, "Tony, I'm not sure I'm excited about that, since God's people don't seem to be doing the job spiritually." Well, in many cases that's true. But there's hope, and in this chapter I want to look further at one of the greatest sources of hope we have: the promise that we can move God's heart and hand through prayer.

If we Christians are going to turn our nation to God, we've got to fall on our knees and our faces before God and pray. We need to not only talk about prayer, but pray. Not only agree on the importance of prayer, but pray. Not only preach on the power of prayer, but pray. To return our nation to its feet, we must first return to our knees.

We're going to base our study for this chapter on a single verse, one that is familiar to most believers: 2 Chronicles 7:14. Whether you're talking about restoring a nation, a city, or a family, this incredible verse holds everything you need to know.

The context of 2 Chronicles 7:14 is very important, because the verse actually continues a sentence that begins in verse 13 and follows God's glory filling the temple. So let's set the stage here.

The occasion is the dedication of Solomon's great temple. Solomon offers a dedicatory prayer in chapter 6 in which he says, in essence, "Lord, I want to lead this people in righteousness. I want to lead this people in honoring You. Lord, I want to do it the way You want it done."

Then in 2 Chronicles 7:1–10, God's glory came down and filled the temple, and the people offered sacrifices and held a feast. Then the text records:

Solomon finished the house of the LORD and the king's palace, and successfully completed all that he had planned on doing in the house of the LORD and in his palace.

Then the LORD appeared to Solomon at night and said to him, "I have heard your prayer and have chosen this place for Myself as a house of sacrifice. If I shut up the heavens so that there is no rain, or if I command the locust to devour the land, or if I send pestilence among My people, and My people who are called by My name humble themselves and pray and seek My face and turn from their wicked ways, then I will hear from heaven, will forgive their sin and will heal their land." (vv. 11–14)

In this hallmark passage, God calls a nation to pray. Prayer is an earthly request for heavenly intervention. It is the tool and strategy that we have been given in order to pull something down from the invisible and into the visible. Prayer enacts God's hand in history like nothing else because prayer is relational communication with God.

The first thing God says in 2 Chronicles 7:14 about those whose prayers get through to Him is that they are "My people who are called by My name." This tells us who can pray. Have you ever wondered why they start off each session of the US Congress with prayer, yet none of this stuff is getting fixed? Why are they always praying down at city hall and in the statehouse, and little happens?

It has to do with whose prayers God hears. When God says "My people" are to pray, He is talking about His covenant people. In the Old Testament, His covenant people were Israel. In the New Testament, it's the church, the body of believers who follow Jesus Christ.

God is not obligated to hear the prayers of sinners, unless they are asking for forgiveness. God has no obligation to sinners who pray because they are not His people and they have not been called by His name.

Only Christians get full access to heaven's ears. Only God's children have access to the throne of grace. If God has decided to allow America to decline, only Christians can make Him rethink that. If God has decided to allow our cities to continue to deteriorate, only Christians can reverse that. Let that truth sink in because it is the foundation of our future.

The principle here is that of representation. That is, only God's appointed representatives get through to Him. His people can get through to Him because they bear His name, which means they are under His authority. When God calls us His people, He is saying, "You belong to Me. You are called to live under My authority."

That's who can pray. And that's why Satan's main goal today is to keep Christians from getting it together, especially on their knees,

> **Satan's big thing is rendering Christians inoperative. If he can lull Christians to sleep spiritually, he's ready to run the show.**

because he knows if we ever get it together, he's in bad shape.

Satan's big thing is rendering Christians inoperative. He's not worried about the sinners. He can handle any sinner because the sinners already belong to him. They don't know they belong to him, but they do. But if he can lull Christians to sleep spiritually, he's ready to run the show.

THE RIGHT ATTITUDE WHEN PRAYING FOR OUR NATION

Beyond our being His people, God says in verse 14 that we need a specific heart attitude when we pray for our country. He's seeking those who will "humble themselves." Humble Christians get through to God. Humility has the idea of dependency. It marks those who understand that without Him, they can do nothing (John 15:5). Too many of us are autonomous and self-sufficient in our own minds. The Bible calls it being "haughty," because we don't really believe that we need God. God is for emergencies only. We say, "God, don't call me. I'll call You."

And so God allows us to go through trials that we can't fix to humble us and to put us flat on our backs, as if to say, "Now let's see you get up all by yourself."

The opposite of God putting you flat on your back is you putting yourself flat on your face before Him in humility. When we kneel, or when we lie prostrate before the Lord, we are demonstrating humility.

God says, "If you want to get My attention, humble yourself. Don't come before Me boastful, proud, and independent, because I will let you know you need Me. I do not need you. Humble yourself." Humility is tied to prayer because prayer is by its nature an admission of our weakness and need. Many Christians don't pray because they are too proud.

You say, "But I'm not proud." If you don't pray you *are* proud, because prayer says to God, "I need You. I can't make this marriage work on my own. I can't solve this problem at work on my own. I am not sufficient in myself to do what needs to be done and to be what You want me to be."

Now if God were to stop the rain today or send locusts or pestilence, most of us would form a committee to study the lack of rain. We would get together a commission to do something about the locusts. We would try everything except the one thing that could change the whole thing: Come before God and pray.

This is why the first challenge we must overcome in bringing about change in our land is to get Christians to bring themselves and their problems before the face of God. To put prayer last means to put God last, and to put God last means everything else we do is a waste of time.

"SEEK MY FACE"

But there are a few elements that can make a prayer more effective than not, and some of those are included in vv. 14–15.

"Seek My face," the Lord tells His people in 2 Chronicles 7:14. This doesn't mean the kind of prayers we usually pray over dinner: "Lord, bless this food to our bodies. In Jesus' name. Amen." Seeking God's face has much more than that in mind.

The context here is one of the people losing focus on God's face, that is, His presence based on His Word. They now have to gain His attention once again by seeking it out. You know how hard it is to carry on a conversation with someone who is not looking at you—maybe they are texting on their phone. God says, essentially, "Stop texting and look at Me." Or, in other words, "Give Me the attention that is due Me."

What has turned the people away from God is sin, so we are the ones who have to come to Him on His terms. Prayer is not a process of negotiation. We don't come before God's face and say, "Now, God, let me tell You what I'm going to do. Let's make a deal."

No, we are the ones without the rain. We are the ones with the locusts. We are the ones whose culture is crum-
bling because of sin and rebellion against

The good news is that God *is* inviting us to seek His face. He is open to our prayers.

God. So we had better be the ones who are
seeking God's terms of reconciliation.

The good news is that God *is* inviting us
to seek His face, to restore fellowship with
Him. He is open to our prayers. We can't
always be sure of that when we alienate an-
other person. He or she might not be willing to reconcile. But God is
always ready for His people to seek His face.

REPENTANCE AND PRAYER

Notice in verse14 that the phrase "seek My face" is closely linked
with "turn from their wicked ways." This is how we seek God's face, by
turning from our sin. The idea here is repentance, turning away from
something that displeases God and turning toward something else that
pleases Him. If you want God to show His face to you, then you must
turn toward Him. And that involves turning away from anything that
is contrary to His will.

The reason our culture is crumbling is that Christians refuse to for-
sake their own secret sins. Marriages are falling apart because Christian
couples refuse to live by God's righteous standards. Christian men
don't want to assume their leadership roles. Christian women want to
define the role of womanhood differently than what God has said in the
Scriptures.

God will not negotiate His standards. He wants us to place ourselves under the authority of His Word and conform to it. Failure to
conform leaves distance from God.

In 2 Chronicles 7, God gives Solomon the essence of the "wicked ways" He is talking about. Speaking of what would happen if Israel ever turned away from Him, God said that if anyone wanted to know why Israel was uprooted from the land (which did happen later), the answer would be: "Because they forsook the Lord, the God of their fathers who brought them from the land of Egypt, and they adopted other gods and worshiped them and served them; therefore He has brought all this adversity on them" (v. 22).

Whenever you pay homage to something or someone other than God, you have created another god. Then God says, "Since that's the god you want, let that god take care of you."

God's people have allowed themselves to be shaped and defined by the culture's standards instead of shaping and defining the culture by God's standards. So we wind up giving God what everybody else is giving Him, which is a polite nod.

But that won't do. Imagine finding out that your teenager is smoking marijuana because "everyone else I know is doing it." That would not be an acceptable reason. Most Christian parents would say, "So what? You are not everyone else. You are my child, and I didn't raise you that way!"

In the same way, God doesn't want His children conforming to what the rest of the world is doing, adopting their standards. He is saying, "You are called by My Name. I'm your Daddy. The rest of the world didn't die on the cross for you. The rest of the world didn't rise from the dead. So the rest of the world shouldn't be telling you what to do."

But the church is accommodating to the culture. Our culture has redefined morality, commitment, and priorities, and we seem powerless to do anything about it simply because it has become too easy and convenient to adopt its ways as our own.

THE RESULT OF PRAYER

There's an important transitional word right in the middle of 2 Chronicles 7:14. "Then," God says, "I will hear from heaven." That means when we as God's people have fulfilled His conditions and come to Him on His terms, then He will hear us—and not until then.

GETTING GOD'S ATTENTION

We know that God hears everything we say. The idea is that He will pay attention to our prayers when we come humbly, seeking His face, and turning from our wicked ways.

It's like when you say to someone, "Didn't you hear what I said?" Yes, that person heard the sounds, but he or she wasn't tuned in to what you were saying. You didn't have the listener's attention.

God says, "If you will come to Me the way that I prescribe, you will have My attention." And more than that, God promises to forgive sin and heal the land when we get His attention. Forgiveness is essential because God is holy. The root meaning of *holy* is that He is separate from everyone and everything else. He is distinct from His creation.

We don't pray to some made-up god who is nothing but the sum total of our experiences and our ideas. Spiritualists want to become one with god by becoming gods. But nobody can become one with God. God is in a class all by Himself.

> Many people think forgiveness means God skips over our sins. No, it's just that Someone else paid the price.

Because of who God is, you can't get past the need for forgiveness. God is distinct from sin. You cannot get God's attention if you go unforgiven. That's why we are told to confess our sins, because God will not listen unless sins are forgiven.

In order for sins to be forgiven, someone must pay the penalty. God does not skip sin. Many people have the idea that forgiveness means God just skips over our sins. No, it's just that Someone else paid the price.

In the Old Testament, animals paid the price. The people had to slay lambs and goats because a holy God demanded that sin had to be paid for. No one gets away with sin. Someone has to pay.

People go to hell because they reject Jesus' payment for sin on the cross, so they have to pay themselves. The reason we can be forgiven is that Jesus Christ has already paid for our sins. And we can keep on being forgiven as believers because the blood of Jesus Christ keeps on forgiving us of our sins as we bring those sins before Him (1 John 1:9).

HEALING OUR LAND

Once God's people are forgiven, then God is free to "heal their land." That is, the effects of their righteousness will spill over to the environment in which they live. This was the way it was supposed to work with Israel. Israel was a special people with a special covenant, and God was to bless all the nations through them as we saw in the water vision in the last chapter (pp. 58–60).

When Israel was right with God, even the Gentiles in their midst were blessed because of Israel's obedience. The healing effects of the promise of 2 Chronicles 7:14 reach beyond individual Christians and even the church to touch the entire society also, as in the case of Nineveh (Jonah 3).

If our culture is to be granted a stay of execution, it will be because God's people are a force for spiritual and emotional healing in our land. If the whole concept of marriage and family is to be salvaged, it will happen when Christians get their marriages and their families lined up with God's commands.

You may say, "My marriage is too far gone." For you maybe, but not for God. When He acts in power, He can change the environment of your marriage.

You may say, "America is too far gone. How are we going to change public education, government, the media?" Well, you change education and government and media by having new people in those places, people who are going to represent Jesus Christ and His frame of reference. That doesn't mean that only Christians are qualified to serve in government or that politics is the primary force of change Christians can work through—but it does mean the political realm is a legitimate sphere of influence for some believers.

By that I mean Christians who are in step with God can use their positions to help transform society. Systems are only bad because the people running the systems are bad. As we move out into society, some of us will be placed in leadership by God, just as Daniel was.

If enough Christians in places of responsibility in medicine, law, government, education, the media, and even the church begin to humble themselves and pray and seek God's face and turn from their wicked ways, we could influence this culture and make the presence of Christ felt from top to bottom and bottom to top.

That's what God is after. He wants people who will commit themselves to Him personally and in their families, and then move out to penetrate the culture for Him.

A BIBLICAL EXAMPLE

Nehemiah, a Jewish exile serving in the court of Artaxerxes, king of Persia, is a classic example of someone who penetrated his culture for God. When he heard about the broken-down condition of Jerusalem, Nehemiah mourned over the city where God's name dwelt.

But Nehemiah also knew how to pray, so he went before God in intense prayer—he called on God, coming to Him humbly with fasting. Nehemiah repented of his sins and the sins of his people, and he sought God's forgiveness and healing for the land of Israel. Notice how his prayer ended in Nehemiah 1:11: "O Lord, I beseech You, may Your ear be attentive to the prayer of Your servant and the prayer of Your servants who delight to revere Your name, and make Your servant successful today, and grant him compassion before this man."

"This man," of course, was King Artaxerxes. Nehemiah could pray for success because things were now in proper perspective. As soon as Nehemiah said amen, he realized that he was "cupbearer to the king" (v. 11). In other words, he was reminded that God had already positioned him to make a difference for his people. That was important because Nehemiah was about to go before the king and make an astounding request. He was getting ready to ask permission to go back and rebuild Jerusalem.

Up to this point, Nehemiah had not made the correlation between being the king's cupbearer and the plight of Jerusalem. But now he realized he was in the most strategic position possible. Artaxerxes was an unsaved and unregenerate man, but the king had the power in his hands to solve Jerusalem's problem.

A person in Nehemiah's position didn't normally ask for time off to go and take care of personal business. As the king's cupbearer, he was the one who daily tasted the royal wine and food before the king partook, so that no one could poison the king.

King Artaxerxes had learned to trust and rely on Nehemiah. The king wasn't going to let him just disappear for months or even years. But Nehemiah had prayed and sought God for his land, and he was willing to put his career on the line to make an impact for God.

Today, many followers of Jesus Christ have separated their careers from their worship; they do not see the kingdom connection between the God they worship and the needs of their culture.

I don't think it has occurred to many Christians that God has strategically positioned them to affect their culture for Him. One way to help rebuild our culture is to "kingdomize" our skills; that is, discover how God can use our so-called secular skills for sacred purposes. Your position of influence may extend to your family, your community, or well beyond that.

Whether your circle is small or large, God can use those who live righteously before Him. Nehemiah's prayer and his life are an example

God not only uses the positions of believers to influence culture. He can use the position of the unrighteous to fulfill His goal.

of 2 Chronicles 7:14 in action. As one called by God, he humbled himself, prayed, and sought God's face.

Let me point out that God does not only use the positions of believers to influence culture. He can use the position of the unrighteous to fulfill His goal for the righteous.

We see this in the description of the Promised Land that we touched on earlier in Deuteronomy 6:10–11. The land God was going to give Israel contained "great and splendid cities which you did not build, and houses full of all good things which you did not fill, and hewn cisterns which you did not dig, vineyards and olive trees which you did not plant."

Do you know how Canaan became such a luxurious land? Do you know how the cisterns were dug? The Hittites and the Amorites and all the others who lived in the land fixed it up for God's people.

SOME QUESTIONS TO ANSWER

As Christians, we need to ask ourselves a couple of questions. Are we going to sit and watch our culture fall apart? Are we going to sit and watch our families disintegrate? Or are we going to do something to turn America to God?

The promise of 2 Chronicles 7:14 is an awesome promise, but you can't enjoy this kind of divine intervention with just a little prayer tossed toward heaven now and then. The kind of prayer that will reclaim lives, families, and a nation for God has to take high priority in our schedules.

In fact, if you look back at Nehemiah 1:4, you will read that Nehemiah prayed and fasted for days when he heard about the conditions in Jerusalem. When you want something from God badly enough, you will push other things aside to seek Him for it.

Nehemiah didn't write out a "Great Society" program for Jerusalem. He didn't propose a Jerusalem "New Deal." He fasted and prayed and sought God, and God revealed His strategy. God was able to reverse years of deterioration in just fifty-two days. Prayer saves time.

We know that God moved in response to Nehemiah's prayer, using the cupbearer's influence with the king to get Artaxerxes to support the rebuilding of Jerusalem. But Nehemiah didn't start with his position. He started with prayer, which created links among God, Nehemiah's problem, and his position.

So let me ask you this: If you see something in your life or in your world that is broken, is prayer the first thing you do, or the last thing you do? If it's the last thing, more than likely, as I said previously, you will have wasted your time on anything else. If prayer comes last, then so will the solution to your problem.

Well, God does not like being last. And if the church is going to help restore America, we can't afford to keep putting Him last. Other things are going to have to wait if we want to turn our communities and nation around. Congregations want to have to come together in a solemn assembly (Joel 1:14) to repent and to throw themselves before the face of Almighty God. Nehemiah was determined that nothing was going to stop him from seeking God and pleading for His favor.

We could save a lot of time running around and worrying if we spent time praying first. You would have to say that in Nehemiah's case, the crumbled walls of Jerusalem were a major problem, something that cried out for immediate and decisive action.

But Nehemiah fasted and prayed first. So my question to you is, What wall is crumbling? The answer: America. The spiritual foundations of this nation are crumbling fast; our beloved nation is imploding upon itself. Political action won't stop the erosion. More money won't stop it.

Yet we have a great God who is willing to forgive and heal our land

…if He can find some people who are ready "to humble themselves and pray and seek (His) face and turn from their wicked ways." When we do that, He can turn the trajectory of our nation around.

6

The Physical
for the Spiritual

Eating is one of the fundamental needs of being human. We eat several times every day to obtain the nourishment and energy we need to survive. Yet every so often, something comes up that is more important than our next meal.

When they're working on a major project, many professionals in the workplace will simply work through their lunch. They don't leave the office nor take a break from working, because the task at hand is more urgent than the meal. Sometimes individuals stay alone at their desks, delaying their meals as they rush to make a deadline. Still others will skip lunch altogether because the task is more important than food. They work right through their lunch hour and continue their task to the end of the day.

It's not just at the office. In many homes, looking after the kids and keeping the house running is such a nonstop job that Mom has no time to sit down and eat. Taking care of her kids' needs and the home is more important than food, and Mom may not even realize that she hasn't eaten anything all day.

What we will do often without thinking because we are busy or distracted, the Lord asks us to do intentionally when He calls us to fast.

THE PRINCIPLE OF FASTING

Let's start with a definition. Fasting is *the deliberate abstinence from some form of physical gratification, for a period of time, in order to achieve a greater spiritual goal.*

We see God's people fast all throughout Scripture when they are in a crisis. When they desperately needed a breakthrough in their circumstances, their emotions, their relationships, their future, or their nation, they fasted.

Fasting shows God that our need for Him is greater than our need for food, or whatever item it is we choose to restrain ourselves from. In Matthew 4, Jesus went into the wilderness to be tested by the Devil. After Jesus prepared by fasting for forty days, the Devil came to Him and tempted Him to eat, but Jesus quoted Deuteronomy 8:3, declaring that man doesn't live on bread alone, but on every word that comes from God.

Fasting is making an intentional choice to place our hunger for God above any other need.

But when we fast, we deliberately show God that we're serious about getting His attention and that we're intently listening for His voice. Skipping a meal is not necessarily fasting.

Fasting is making an intentional choice to place our hunger for God above any other need.

Remember what Jesus said to the Devil? We can't live on just food because we need the Word of God even more. Fasting shows God and ourselves that His Word is more important than food. When we fast, we give the Holy Spirit our full attention.

Zechariah 7:5–6 tells us that when we eat, we do it for ourselves. But when we fast, we do it for the Lord.

When we fast this way we demonstrate our great need for God. It leads to a brokenness that shouts, "I can't do this!" The self-sufficient man or woman won't fast, but the desperate one will. The self-sufficient church won't fast, but the desperate one will. The self-sufficient nation won't fast, but the desperate one will.

The truth is we cannot live the Christian life in our own strength. We can't make things happen. We can't force a revival simply by strategizing one. We've got to starve our flesh to feed our spirit. When our spirits are strong and our flesh is weak, huge spiritual breakthroughs explode all over. Isaiah 58:6–9 promises that when we fast the way God intended, our light will shine, healing will come quickly to our land, and the Lord will answer when we call. The question is not whether fasting makes a difference. The question is, "How bad do we want a difference to be made?"

When you fast, you say no to yourself so you can hear yes from God in a time of need or crisis.

Fasting usually involves setting aside food, although we can fast from any physical appetite, including sex within marriage (1 Corinthians 7:35). Another thing we could fast from are the hours we spend watching television or surfing the Internet. The idea is to devote the time we would ordinarily spend on these activities to prayer and waiting before the Lord. Fasting calls us to renounce the natural in order to invoke the supernatural. When you fast, you say no to yourself so you can hear yes from God in a time of need or crisis. Our nation is in a time of crisis—a collective fast throughout the body of Christ on behalf of our land sends a message to our Lord that we are wanting and waiting to hear from Him.

As I said earlier, fasting is a recurring principle throughout the

Bible. People in Scripture often fasted in situations that demanded a spiritual breakthrough. Recall God's words to Zecharaiah: "Say to all the people of the land and to the priests, 'When you fasted and mourned in the fifth and seventh months these seventy years, was it actually for Me that you fasted? When you eat and drink, do you not eat for yourselves and do you not drink for yourselves?'" (7:5–6).

Even though the fasts God referred to here would have been unnecessary if His people had repented, these verses still give us an important principle about fasting. When we eat, we eat for ourselves, with nothing more than our own satisfaction in mind. But when we fast, we should do so with God in mind, for His pleasure.

As the passage indicates, we become servants to the cry of our flesh to receive food. We eat for ourselves. But when we fast, God says, "This is for Me." Just as food satisfies us, fasting satisfies God because we are saying to Him, "The cry of my soul for You is greater than the cry of my stomach for food or anything else."

To understand the impact of fasting you need to understand the reason behind it. God created Adam out of the dust from the ground. It wasn't until God breathed into Adam's nostrils the breath of life that he became "a living being" (Genesis 2:7). Your ultimate value is not in your body, but in your soul. It's the nonmaterial part of us that is in God's image, not our bodies.

What do we do so often? We feed the body while starving the soul. But when we fast, we give the soul a higher priority than the body. We are asking God to interact with our souls with regard to a spiritual matter.

This is the principle of fasting. The question is, Are you willing to give up the feeding of your flesh in order to gain spiritual riches in our land?

THE PURPOSE OF FASTING

Let's talk about the why of fasting. According to Isaiah 58:4, the purpose of fasting is "to make your voice heard on high." When we fast with the proper motivation, our voice is heard in heaven. That is, we come into God's presence in a powerful way. If that is the purpose, then imagine what kind of voice we could have in heaven if we were to come together across class, ethnic, and denominational boundaries to collectively fast and call on God to intervene in our nation.

The nature of fasting is such that it demands concentrated effort and time to come into God's presence. Think about the effort we make to eat when we're hungry. Most of us will make a way where there is no way when it's mealtime. Why? Because we are desperate to satisfy our hunger. But when we fast, we are desperate to satisfy something much deeper—a spiritual need. We are desperate to make our voices heard on high.

Something unique happens when we fast. God sharpens our spiritual focus so we can see things more clearly. In 1 Thessalonians 5:23, Paul prayed that his readers would be sanctified and preserved in their "spirit and soul and body." Paul's order here is purposeful. We are not made up of body, soul, and spirit, but spirit, soul, and body. We are created to live from the inside out, not from the outside in.

You say, "Why is that important?" Because if you look at yourself as a body that happens to house a soul and a spirit, you will live for your body first. But if you understand that you are spirit at the core of your being, you will live for the spirit.

Your spirit is the part of you that enables you to communicate with God. It gives you God-awareness. Your soul enables you to communicate with yourself. It gives you self-awareness. Your body enables you to communicate with your environment. It gives you other-awareness.

We need to live from our spirit out to our bodies. The reason so many people have messed-up bodies is because they have messed-up souls. And the reason they have messed-up souls is because their spirits are not under the control of the Holy Spirit. If we want to really live, the spirit, or the inner person, must be set free. Our spirits must be cracked open to release the Spirit's life, and fasting helps us do this.

Far too often, our problem is that we aren't ready for God to work in our spirit. We make all kinds of resolutions and promises, which are really just ways of saying to God, "I can do this myself." But if we could do it, we would have already done it. We have more Christian organizations in our country than ever before, more churches than ever before, more Christian radio and television than ever before, and certainly more Christian books than ever before—but our nation is farther from God today, collectively, than we've ever been before. One of the primary reasons for this is that we have become a nation of self-sufficient programs and people who refuse to humble ourselves collectively before the Lord. When we fast and pray and seek His movement in our spirits, we are humbling ourselves.

What God wants to hear us say is, "Lord, we can't do this. We've tried everything we know and we can't fix our land. Lord, we throw our inability and our failure at Your feet."

God says, "Now I can do something."

Fasting demonstrates to God that we are setting aside the flesh in order to deal with the spirit.

Otherwise we wind up trying to live the Christian life in our own power. We call on our flesh to help us defeat the flesh—which is a contradiction in terms. We need to set aside our fleshly efforts and focus on the spirit. Fasting is a tangible way of demonstrating to God that we are setting aside the flesh in order to deal with the spirit.

More than that, fasting is also a way of prostrating ourselves before God. In the Bible, when people were broken before the Lord they often fell on their faces. They put ashes on their heads and tore their clothes as a way of saying, "Lord, I can't do anything. I am at the end of my rope."

God wants us to reach that point so He can demonstrate His power and get all the glory, which He deserves. The apostle James says those who humble themselves before God will be lifted up (James 4:10). Fasting puts us on the path of humility.

The question in fasting is, How badly do you want an answer? How much do you want deliverance? How badly do you want to save your country not only for ourselves but for the future generations? Do you want it enough to give up food or some other gratification?

You may feel like giving up on the problems plaguing us in our land today, but if you haven't fasted over it yet, you haven't done everything you can do. You have one more option—to throw yourself on the mercy of God in humility while giving up a craving of the flesh for a greater need of the spirit.

The bottom line is when we fast, we will get God's undivided attention: "You will call, and the Lord will answer; You will cry, and He will say, 'Here I am'" (Isaiah 58:9).

You may say, "But I've been calling to God all this time." Are you calling to Him with the fast? Remember, fasting makes your voice heard on high. God wants to be treated seriously.

A BIBLICAL EXAMPLE OF A NATIONAL FAST

We need to fast for our nation for a number of reasons. One is the fact that Satan seeks to destroy a nation to destroy its people. His purpose is "to steal and kill and destroy" (John 10:10).

We also need protection from evil people who are being used by Satan to carry out his agenda. Now don't misunderstand. People themselves are not the enemy. The Devil behind the people energizing them to do evil is the enemy. But we need protection from the attitudes and actions of people who seek the demise of Christians and Christian values as well as the demise of God's kingdom work.

In the Bible, we often find people fasting when they were surrounded by their enemies, under a dire threat of destruction, facing Satan and his demonic realm, and overcome by fear.

One of these instances is the story of Esther, which tells of a time when God's people sought Him through fasting and presumably also through prayer in a time of terrible crisis.

Let me briefly set the context for our study of Esther. She was the beautiful young Jewish exile in the kingdom of Persia who was chosen by King Ahasuerus to become queen. Esther became the king's favorite, but the key to the plot is that no one in the Persian court knew Esther was a Jew.

Esther had an older Jewish relative named Mordecai, who served as her guardian in Persia. While Esther was finding favor with the king, Mordecai fell into disfavor with Haman, the king's top adviser. Haman was a cruel man who came to hate Mordecai bitterly when the latter refused to bow down to Haman like everyone else did. To bow to Haman would have been a violation of God's law, and Mordecai refused to do it.

Haman's hatred was so intense that he wasn't content just to kill Mordecai (Esther 3:6). Haman convinced King Ahasuerus that the whole Jewish race was made up of disloyal troublemakers who were bad news for his kingdom. So at Haman's prompting, the king signed an edict calling for the slaughter of all Jews in Persia on a given day. That's how evil is. Satan doesn't want just you. He wants all of the Christians in our country.

Talk about evil people manipulated by Satan. The Devil was clever, because he knew Persian law could never be changed once it had been enacted. In other words, there was no human way to undo Haman's decree. Haman became Satan's tool to achieve his number one goal, the total destruction of God's people.

So all the Jews in Persia were now under a death sentence, and this is where we pick up the story. Mordecai went into mourning, and Esther sent a servant to find out why. Mordecai sent back a copy of the king's edict with the message, "You've got to do something. Go to the king and plead for the lives of your people. You're a Jew, and you'll die too if Haman's edict is carried out."

All of this leads to the climactic passage in Esther 4 that I want to examine. When Esther got the bad news, she sent a message back to Mordecai, which I'll summarize.

"Mordecai, anyone who goes in to the king without being called will be put to death unless the king decides otherwise. If I go to the king now to appeal for the Jews, I'll be killed, because he hasn't called for me for the past thirty days" (v. 11).

Esther was saying, "Mordecai, I know I'm a Jew, and I know you used to be my guardian and I do love you. But you can't expect me to risk my life for you. If I go in to see Ahasuerus, I might die."

Esther was afraid, and for good reason. She was gripped with fear because she knew the rules of the house, and she didn't want to die. As far as she could see, there was no one to protect her from the king's wrath.

But the Jews in Persia also needed protection. So Mordecai sent this word back to Esther:

Do not imagine that you in the king's palace can escape any more than all the Jews. For if you remain silent at this time, relief and deliverance will arise for the Jews from another place and you and your father's house will perish. And who knows whether you have not attained royalty for such a time as this? (Esther 4:13–14)

Mordecai wanted Esther to understand that she had not been chosen queen just because she was so pretty that Ahasuerus couldn't take his eyes off her. God had made her the queen "for such a time as this," for this time when His people were being threatened with annihilation.

Esther needed to understand the theology of this situation. That is, she needed to see things from God's perspective. Mordecai's theological response showed her the truth. Esther was afraid, but she also saw that God could use her to protect her people from Haman.

So Esther addressed her fear by sending this message back to Mordecai:

> Go, assemble all the Jews who are found in Susa, and fast for me; do not eat or drink for three days, night or day. I and my maidens also will fast in the same way. And thus I will go in to the king, which is not according to the law; and if I perish, I perish. (v. 16)

As the queen of Persia, Esther called for all of the Jews in a certain region to collectively fast. When her people were at stake and the problem was too far gone for her to handle on her own, she turned to the only solution that could possibly work—appealing to God in the utmost of humility and dependency—a collective fast.

She was asking much of people—asking them to come together for one purpose, to renounce food while asking God for mercy.

Her request involved Mordecai and all the Jews in the Persian capital of Susa. She was asking much of a lot of people—asking those across social spheres to come together for one purpose, to renounce food while asking God for mercy.

In America today, we cannot solve the issues that we face in crime, education disparity, economic fraility, the redefinition of the family, and moral failures. Despite our best efforts, this is beyond us. That is why we must, as a collective group of Christians, come before the Lord in a collective fast to seek His hand and intervention in our land. To seek His wisdom in our hearts. To seek His guidance in what we are to do to turn a nation to God.

When Esther called for a collective fast, she got it. Esther 4:17 is an important verse: "So Mordecai went away and did just as Esther had commanded him." Why is this verse significant? Because just a few verses earlier, Esther was afraid. She didn't want to risk her position or livelihood to do anything on behalf of her people. As a result, Mordecai was telling her what to do. Yet now Esther was commanding Mordecai and everybody else to fast. In other words, Esther had stopped being a fearful victim. She was no longer controlled by her fear. She was no longer victimized by Haman or her circumstances.

When you're a victim of fear, your circumstances dictate your response. Everyone but God can tell you what to do. But when you tap into God's power by fasting, He steps in.

You can read the rest of the story. You may already know how it ends. Esther arranged a private banquet with herself, the king, and Haman, at which she revealed Haman's plot and the fact that she and her people were going to be killed. Haman was condemned to death without even having the chance to speak in his own defense (Esther 7:1–10).

The bottom line is that Haman was hanged and the Jews were allowed the right to arm and defend themselves. On the day appointed for their slaughter, they routed their enemies and won a great victory.

When you seek God and His intervention, He will "make your enemies your footstool" (Psalm 110:1). Through a collective time of fasting and praying, we are appealing to a greater power, and God has the ability to rearrange circumstances. We have a powerful foe in Satan who wants nothing more than to destroy any and all Christian influence in our land and around the world, but we serve the King of kings and Lord of lords. When we make our appeal to Him, it doesn't matter how powerful the enemy may be.

It is time that we heed Esther's example—recognize that the issues in front of us are too big for us to overcome on our own, and we send out the clarion call for a collective time of fasting and prayer throughout America.

When we engage the church in a fast—together, we will begin the process of becoming equipped to fortify and strengthen our great land.

THE CHOICE

A man once became lost in the desert. His throat was parched, and he knew he wouldn't live much longer if he didn't get some water.

Just then off in the distance he saw a little old shack. He made his way to the shack and found a pump inside with a jug of water sitting next to it. He reached for the jug to take a drink only to find this note on the jug: "The pump will give you all the water you need. But in order to prime the pump, you must pour in all the water in the jug."

This man had a dilemma. Should he drink the water in the jug and then be out of water and perhaps be unable to get more, or should he believe the note and use the water he had to prime the pump? Would the jug even have enough water to prime the pump?

He began to think through his choices. "Suppose I pour all my water in the pump and nothing happens? I not only lose the water; I may lose my life.

"On the other hand, if there is a well underneath this pump and I use the water to prime it, then I can get all the water I need."

This thirsty man's dilemma is the question we have to ask ourselves as disciples. Do we get all we can get now because there might not be much later, or do we give up what we can get now because of all that's available if we are willing to take the risk of committing ourselves to Christ?

The man thought for a moment and then decided to take the risk. He poured the contents of the jug into the pump and began to work the handle. Sweat broke out on his forehead as nothing happened at first.

But as he pumped a few drops of water appeared, and then came a huge gush. He drank all he wanted, took a bath, then filled up every other container he could find in the shack.

Because he was willing to give up momentary satisfaction, the man got all the water he needed. Now the note also said, "After you have finished, please refill the jug for the next traveler." The man refilled the jug, then added to the note, "Please prime the pump. Believe me, it works."

We need to prime the pump. Some of us are half-stepping on Christ. We're trying to live in two worlds at the same time. We want to be sacred and secular, worldly and spiritual. We want to love God and love this world order. But my charge to you to remember is this: You can have the world if you want it—you just can't have the world *and* God.

You have to pour all the water—give God everything you have—if you want God to pour His covenantal blessings back on you. Only in the domain of the kingdom will you discover God's abundance and power to experience victory in your own life. And only as we in the church make seeking God's face through prayer and fasting a high value will we experience the renewal in our nation that we all so deeply want.

7

The Greatest
Of These

Several years ago I pulled into a service station to fill up my car with gas. I put the nozzle in the opening of my tank, filled it up, paid the cashier, and then went on my way. It wasn't too long after I started driving that I began to hear some unusual sounds coming from the back of my car. In addition to that, my car began to jerk a bit and sputter.

I looked at my dashboard and saw that my tank was full, and that the indicator lights did not reveal that anything was wrong—yet my car continued to slow down, and those jerking movements continued. While I was still able to drive, I decided to take my car straight to the mechanic. After he had a moment to check it out, I asked him if there was something wrong with my engine or transmission. He just smiled and said, "Tony, I think you made a mistake."

"What do you mean?" I asked.

"Well, when everything looked fine under the hood and everything tested fine as far as the parts were concerned, I decided to sample your fuel. And it appears that you put the wrong fuel in your car. You are never going to get anywhere when you have the wrong stuff inside."

Friends, it's easy to think that doing the right thing by going through the right motions is all that we need to do. It's easy to come up with a formula, carry it out, and then expect everything to run smoothly. If God says to fast, we fast. If God says to pray, we pray. If God says to go to church, we go to church. If God says to have a national solemn assembly, we have a national solemn assembly.

Until we have the right stuff deep within—the living Spirit of God— we will continue to merely bump along.

But in the midst of the motions, we dare not forget that what is on the inside is what matters most. Going to church and filling up on good music, worship, fellowship, and the Word is good, but until we have the right stuff down deep within—the living Spirit of God—we will continue to merely bump along, not getting very far at all.

One of my greatest concerns in seeking to call the body of Christ into a time of both a corporate and national solemn assembly is that we will focus too much on the what, where, why, and when that we will forget about the how.

THE HEART OF THE MATTER

We will focus too much on the mechanics and miss the heart. I can hear you now. "But Tony, didn't you just tell us that we needed to pray and fast as the body of Christ?" Yes, I did. But that's not all we need to do, and here's why. I've been leading our local body of Christ in an annual week-long solemn assembly for decades. It is a tradition that begins our new year off with an intentional focus on God. Yet in all of these decades, I've seen people miss the heart of the matter time and time again.

Yes, they go through the motions. Yes, they skip the food, television, entertainment, music, or whatever it is they choose to fast from.

Yes, they ask the Lord for the breakthrough they so desire in their lives. But in the end, they don't receive it. They are no better off than before the week-long solemn assembly began. Fast forward another year and things seem even worse than before in their lives. I've seen this happen far too many times.

Sometimes frustrated congregants will come up to me and ask, "Pastor, I've gone through the solemn assembly four years in a row, and yet I still haven't gotten my breakthrough. What am I doing wrong?" After further discussion, the conversation usually ends up in a similar vein as the others who ask—on the heart. The reason for this is simple—a consecrated time of solemn assembly, of prayer and fasting before the Lord must begin from within where we align our hearts with the very heart of God. It can't just be something we attend and cross off of our list, despite our best intentions. It's not about clocking in and clocking out. It's not about the actions. It's not even about the words we say, the prayers we pray, or the songs we sing.

It's all about the heart, for out of the heart flows the wellsprings of life (Proverbs 4:23).

It's about our hearts being filled with the right stuff—the very Spirit of God's own heart Himself. When we have His heart, our inward thoughts and our outward actions will naturally reflect Him (1 John 4:16). When we have His heart, our prayers will be answered (Psalm 37:4; John 15:7). He has promised us this in His Word.

ISRAEL'S FAST IN FUTILITY

The people of Israel would often enter into a fast or solemn assembly to seek the Lord during biblical times. Yet they did not always experience His presence or power in response to their actions. Because God was so clear in letting them know why He did not respond to their fast, we can avoid fasting in futility by paying attention to what God said—recorded in the Scriptures—and applying it to our own personal and national situations. When we do this, we will experience God's response to us in a positive and life-changing manner.

The most vivid biblical account of God's nonresponse to fasting is recorded in Isaiah 58. The Israelites had begun to complain that they had fasted with no response at all. It says, "Why have we fasted and You do not see? Why have we humbled ourselves and You do not notice?" (v. 3).

In other words, the Israelites wanted to know why they had gone to all of the effort and sacrifice of skipping their lamb, leavened bread, and potatoes if God wasn't even going to notice. They wanted to know that since they had done their part, why God had not kept up His end of the bargain. They'd missed their meals. They'd bowed their heads. They'd read their Bibles, sung their songs of praise—gone through all of the correct religious actions and activities. And yet God had not noticed. According to them, He had not seen at all.

Maybe you've experienced a similar thing. You've fasted and prayed for a mate, a child, yourself, your job—our nation . . . and yet you've seen no improvement, no breakthrough. It's as if God didn't even take note. You are like the people of Israel standing before Him and asking, "I did my part; why aren't You doing Yours?" And so you hesitate to do it again.

God let His people know that religious rituals without an authentic spiritual relationship was a waste of time.

Yet God's response to the nation of Israel is His response to us as well.

Through Isaiah, God let His people know that fulfilling religious rituals when there was no authentic spiritual relationship was a waste of both effort and time. Participating in external, albeit legitimate, religious activities (fasting, prayer, reading Scripture, etc.) without the internal relational reality with God Himself just didn't cut it.

The Israelites in Isaiah 58 were doing a lot of the right things. To those around them, they looked like churchgoing, Bible-believing followers of God. They were fasting, praying, worshiping, fellowshiping, and reading God's Scriptures at the temple. Even God acknowledges that they were seeking Him (Isaiah 58:2). Yet after this acknowledgment, He lets them know that He knows why they were seeking Him and it is because of this that their fast was not bringing about the results they desired. We read, "Behold, on the day of your fast you find *your* desire, and drive hard all your workers. Behold, you fast for contention and strife and to strike with a wicked fist" (vv. 3–4, italics added).

THE WRONG MOTIVE, AND THE RIGHT ONE

Basically, God let them know that the motivation behind their fast was personal gain, not His glory. He tells them that their horizontal relationship with others, which was in disrepair, revealed the true nature of their hearts. Essentially, a heart aligned with God will reflect God's nature—and God's nature is one of justice, equity, faithfulness, forgiveness, kindness, and love.

We read in 1 John 4:8 this very thing. It says, "The one who does not love does not know God, for God is love." Love, described for us by Paul in his letter to the church at Corinth,

> never gives up. Love cares more for others than for self. Love doesn't want what it doesn't have. Love doesn't strut, doesn't have a swelled head, doesn't force itself on others, isn't always "me first." Doesn't fly off the handle, doesn't keep score of the sins of others, doesn't revel when others grovel, takes pleasure in the flowering of truth, puts up with anything, trusts God always, always looks for the best, never looks back, but keeps going to the end. Love never dies. (1 Corinthians 13:4–8, THE MESSAGE)

That is the definition of God's heart: Love—the compassionate and righteous pursuit of the well-being of others. The writer of the book of Hebrews tells us that Jesus Christ is the "exact representation" of God's nature (Hebrews 1:3). Jesus modeled love in all that He did. Therefore, as disciples of Christ living in the church age today, we are to be reflections of Him who reflects the Father. We are to be people of love. That is to be our motive in all we do.

I like to explain it this way. As an outgrowth of our vertical relationship with God, we are to be the visible manifestation of the horizontal Jesus to others. When we are not, something is amiss in the vertical. And when something is amiss in the vertical, our fasting—like the Israelites despite their zeal and efforts—will remain futile.

Fasting is about much more than simply refraining from food. It's about filling our hearts with that which fills God's own, and then letting that love overflow.

THE FAST THAT IS *NOT* ACCEPTABLE TO GOD

God let the Israelites know through the prophet Isaiah that yes, they were doing all of the correct and seemingly zealous things—but that it was ritual and not relational. Because if it truly were relational in nature, then their hearts would connect with His own, and as a natural outgrowth, their hearts and their actions would reflect His love. But they didn't reflect Him at all. Instead He found within them contention and selfish desires (Isaiah 58:3–4).

In verse 5 of Isaiah 58, God asks them about the fast they have chosen when He says through the prophet, "Is it a fast like this which I choose, a day for a man to humble himself? Is it for bowing one's head like a reed and for spreading out sackcloth and ashes as a bed? Will you call this a fast, even an acceptable day to the Lord?"

By all appearances, that sounds correct. Shouldn't we fast by bowing our heads like a reed? Shouldn't we spread out sackcloth and ashes? Doesn't that sound like an acceptable thing to do? Any cursory glance over Isaiah 58:5 might lead the reader to believe that this is what God is asking them to do.

But it is not.

God says that it is not the fast He is asking them to do; rather, that is the fast they themselves want to do. After all, a reed merely bows to the wind—it only conforms to outward circumstances and influences. A reed never bows from within. Bowing like a reed is akin to ceremonial worship. And sitting on sackcloth and ashes only brings about a spectacle to those around it.

Throughout Scripture, the Lord reminds us that He is not impressed with our spectacles or with our outward actions at all:

For You do not delight in sacrifice, otherwise I would give it; You are not pleased with burnt offering. The sacrifices of God are a broken spirit; a broken and a contrite heart, O God, You will not despise. (Psalm 51:16–17)

"What are your multiplied sacrifices to Me?" says the Lord. "I have had enough of burnt offerings of rams and the fat of fed cattle; and I take no pleasure in the blood of bulls, lambs, or goats." (Isaiah 1:11)

And He [Jesus] also told this parable to some people who trusted in themselves that they were righteous, and viewed others with contempt: "Two men went up into the temple to pray, one a Pharisee and the other a tax collector. The Pharisee stood and was praying this to himself: 'God, I thank You that I am not like other people: swindlers, unjust, adulterers, or even like this tax collector. I fast twice a week; I pay tithes of all that I get.' But the tax collector, standing some distance away, was even unwilling to lift up his eyes to heaven, but was beating his breast, saying, 'God, be merciful to me, the sinner!' I tell you, this man went to his house justified rather than the other; for everyone who exalts himself will be humbled, but he who humbles himself will be exalted." (Luke 18:9–14)

For I delight in loyalty rather than sacrifice, and in the knowledge of God rather than burnt offerings. (Hosea 6:6)

Has the Lord as much delight in burnt offerings and sacrifices as in obeying the voice of the Lord? Behold, to obey is better than sacrifice, and to heed than the fat of rams. (1 Samuel 15:22)

What is it that God has asked us to obey and to heed? Jesus told us when He answered the Pharisees' question of what was the greatest commandment—the greatest thing that we could obey. He didn't answer with one command, but two when He said, "You shall love the Lord your God with all your heart, and with all your soul, and with all your mind. This is the great and foremost commandment. The second is like it. You shall love your neighbor as yourself. On these two commandments depend the whole Law and the Prophets" (Matthew 22:37–40). In other words, do these two things and you will obey everything else as well simply by default.

THE FAST THAT *IS* ACCEPTABLE TO GOD

Through the prophet Isaiah, God shared these same truths with the Israelites in this way when He told them the kind of fast that is acceptable to Him:

Is this not the fast which I choose, to loosen the bonds of wickedness, to undo the bands of the yoke, and to let the oppressed go free and break every yoke? Is it not to divide your bread with the hungry and bring the homeless poor into the house; when you see the naked, to cover him; and not to hide yourself from your own flesh?" (Isaiah 58:6–7)

Essentially, the fast that God chooses can be summed up in one word: *Love*. It is done in seeking the welfare and good of one another. In loosening the bonds of wickedness that keep so many in a state of despair. In undoing the bands of the yoke and letting the oppressed go free. Or as the prophet Micah put it, "He has told you, O man, what is good; and what does the Lord require of you but to do justice, to love kindness, and to walk humbly with your God?" (Micah 6:8).

The fast God requires is a fast of kindness, love, service, giving . . . mercy, and humility.

In other words, to divide our bread with the hungry. To bring the homeless poor into our house. To cover the naked. To care for our families—these are the things the Lord asks. This is the fast He requires—it is a fast of kindness, love, service, giving, personal restraint, forgiveness, mercy, and humility. It is a fast of going into our communities and into our schools and being a mother to the motherless and a father to the fatherless through mentoring. It is a fast of tutoring, teaching, loving, inspiring, and lifting those held down by a social system of inequity and bringing them up to the level of their destinies. It is a fast of compassion. A fast of helping those in need, whether those needs be physical, spiritual, or emotional in nature.

Yes, it is far easier to simply bow the head and sit on some ashes. It is easier to call together a gathering where we confess a few sins, promise to not do them again, and ask God for our breakthroughs.

Yet that is not what God is asking us to do, at least not only that. God says clearly that the fast He wants is a fast of intentional love—love in action. When we do those things, coupled with a heart of humble contrition before the Lord for our individual, familial, and corporate sins, He says He will do His part in bringing power, life, and healing to us and to our land.

Isaiah goes on to give the benefits of fasting God's way. As you read it, notice the conditional statements in it—the if/then scenarios that clearly lay out for us what we are to do "if" we want to experience the "then." When we fast with intentional love:

> *Then* your light will break out like the dawn, and your recovery will speedily spring forth; and your righteousness will go before you; the glory of the Lord will be your rear guard. *Then* you will call, and the Lord will answer; you will cry, and He will say, "Here I am." *If* you remove the yoke from your midst, the pointing of the finger and speaking wickedness, and *if* you give yourself to the hungry and satisfy the desire of the afflicted, *then* your light will rise in darkness and your gloom will become like midday. And the Lord will continually guide you, and satisfy your desire in scorched places, and give strength to your bones; and you will be like a watered garden, and like a spring of water whose waters do not fail. Those from among you will rebuild the ancient ruins; you will raise up the age-old foundations; and you will be called the repairer of the breach, the restorer of the streets in which to dwell. (Isaiah 58:8–12, italics added)

Friends and fellow citizens, do we want the light of the body of Christ to break out like the dawn across our nation? Do we want our country to experience a speedy recovery from what plagues it? Do we want God's guidance in our healthcare, economics, and education? Do we want to repair the breach and restore our churches, cities, and our country?

If the answer to any of those questions is yes, then we have to do the "if" that comes before it. It's dependent on that. Because the fast that will get God's attention is a fast to love others in both word and action. To stop pointing the fingers at those we don't agree with in a different political party, denomination, or cultural context. To stop speaking wickedness and judgment against those we don't like. To replace berating with winning people to Jesus Christ through compassion and kindness. To help the oppressed go free—rather than condemn them through what we say. To clothe the naked, rather than expose them or watch them on the Internet when no one else is looking. To satisfy the desire of the afflicted rather than ignore them as we satisfy our own desires instead. We are to do all of this, however, without compromising truth or biblical standards.

God's fast isn't quite as easy as skipping a meal or saying a prayer, although as we saw in the last chapter, doing those things are part and partial to His fast. But if we only do those things and not couple them with intentional acts of love, we will not get His results.

In order to influence our country for good and turn our nation to God, we—His people—must fast with His heart. For only when we have His heart, will we invoke His hand.

8

Igniting the Fire of Revival

We don't normally suffer from cold weather here in Texas. Our winters are typically mild, with temperatures rarely dipping into single digits. As a lover of hot weather—I've been known to drive in Dallas in the middle of July without using my air conditioner while putting my windows down—I appreciate this aspect of where I live. The cold has never suited me too well.

However, there are those times when a winter cold front heads south, bringing snow, sleet, and ongoing misery. It was during one of these occasions that our heater stopped working in our home. The weather outside snarled with a biting wind but the temperature inside bit back. It was cold.

I called the repairman who quickly showed up at our house. As he examined our heater, I made the comment that it looked like it was time to get a new heater. Lois and I live in the same home we've lived in for some forty years. Anyone who owns a home for that long can relate to how many "projects" and weekend to-do lists pop up. Things get old, wear out, and need attending to. I just assumed that this was another one of those things.

Knowing that it would take a day or two to get the new heater, Lois had notified our grown-up kids who were visiting. But after the repairman made his way through the intricacies of our heater, he turned to me and shook his head.

"You don't need a new heater," he said. "This one is just fine. Your problem is with your igniter. Your igniter is not sending the message to ignite the flame so that you can get fire to engage the other parts."

The repairman's diagnosis saved us money on a new heater we did not need. It also saved us the time of waiting on an entirely new unit, because when he replaced the igniter, what had been a bad situation turned around suddenly. Immediately. It didn't take all that I had thought it would take to bring the flame of fire to the heater and turn my situation around.

THE FIRE THAT IGNITES

What we are facing in our nation today are the biting temperatures exuding from the coldness of hearts toward God. The results that have shown up in our land may look insurmountable. We may assume that since this has been going on for so long, we need to replace the whole thing—create new programs, spend a lot of money, and disrupt people's lives. But it doesn't take long to get things right when God is in the equation. When the fire of His Holy Spirit is loosed to ignite lives—we will experience the impact suddenly. The Holy Spirit is the fire that ignites.

In Scripture, fire is a symbol often used in relationship to God. God is called a "consuming fire" (Hebrews 12:29). Elsewhere He uses fire to manifest His presence in the burning bush (Exodus 3:2), Ezekiel's vision (Ezekiel 1:4), and in what is known as His Shekinah glory (see 2 Chronicles 7:13; Ezekiel 10:4, 18–19). In the books of Judges and

1 Kings, we read about fire as a sign of God's power (13:20; 18:38). And in His preeminent introduction to His works among and within mankind, the Holy Spirit manifests Himself as blazing tongues of fire (Acts 2:3).

In this middle section of the book, we have walked through the steps we need to take in order to seek God's hand in turning our nation to Him. We began by looking at the importance of prayer followed up with a discourse on fasting. The previous chapter looked at God's ideal fast, which involves the greatest commandment, "the greatest of these"—love. When all three of these elements align within our lives and our corporate body, we can expect the full power of God's Holy Spirit to light His fire in our land.

No discussion on revival, sacred gatherings, or solemn assemblies in the church age would be complete without a focused examination of this primary igniter of change, the Spirit. And no discussion on the Holy Spirit would be complete without a look at what He did to usher in revival shortly after Jesus Christ ascended into heaven.

THE POWER OF THE SPIRIT

Just before He returned to heaven, Jesus told the disciples who had lived with Him and learned from Him for three solid years that they were to do nothing at all until they received the Spirit's power. The power of the Spirit is very real, and it accessible to each of us. Jesus said, "But you shall receive power when the Holy Spirit has come upon you; and you shall be My witnesses both in Jerusalem, and in all Judea and Samaria, and even to the remotest part of the earth" (Acts 1:8).

The clear implication of Jesus' words here is that the disciples would not have power until the Spirit came: Power is not simply a concept to be understood but a reality to be experienced. It was Christ's commission that these individuals change not only their local community and nation, but also their world for good. However, Christ knew they could not pull off His intended program without His Spirit. So He told them to wait.

After all, the disciples were a weak group of men. Peter had denied Jesus. The other disciples left Him because they feared the Jews. They ran and hid until the Spirit came. But when the Spirit came upon them, those weak-kneed men who had run when the going got tough received their spiritual courage. They got the Holy Spirit's power, the Holy Spirit's difference.

Their courage and power didn't come because of changes in their environment. The difference was the Holy Spirit. That's why Jesus had told them to wait. Yet when the "tongues of fire" touched the men and ignited within them a strength beyond their own, they became drastically changed.

Something happened in particular to the apostle Peter. According to Acts 4:13, the Jewish authorities marveled at the courage shown by Peter—and John too. Those authorities knew both were "uneducated." I like that because it means they hadn't been to a formal school. But they had the power of the Spirit.

The Spirit of God makes the truth of God real in the hearts of men.

The power of the Holy Spirit has nothing to do with the degrees you have on your wall. It has nothing to do with your theological training or background. You can have it all and still lack influence. But if you have the power of the Holy Spirit, somebody else is going to know it. If you have the fire of the Spirit, it's going to become evident that something powerful is at work in you.

When Peter and the apostles began to proclaim the message of the kingdom to the people at Pentecost, those in attendance began to hear and understand "the mighty deeds of God" about which they spoke. In fact, they understood what they said even in their own different languages. The Holy Spirit translated their words into other languages spoken by people of other nations. What God had done at Babel—a confusion of the language between those who sought to make a name for themselves apart from Him—He did the opposite of that at Pentecost through the power of the Holy Spirit. These men sought to expand God's name and influence through their speech, and the Holy Spirit acted as interpreter to those in attendance, as He does still to this day in a variety of ways.

It is the job of the Spirit of God to make the truth of God real in the hearts of people. The only way to successfully impact and transform our nation for good will be through the Holy Spirit's power. We do not possess enough skills, talents or power on our own to carry this out. We need the Holy Spirit now just as much as He was needed at Pentecost.

LIFTED TO A WHOLE NEW LEVEL

How do you know when the Holy Spirit has set fire to a church or a nation for revival? Because the collective impact of the individuals within it is manifested in ways that are not natural to history, background, orientation, or even skills—and because the Holy Spirit has lifted them up to a whole new level of power.

This is similar to when you fill a balloon with helium—since it is full of something designed to take it above ground level, the gas-filled balloon soars upward. The same thing happens to the church and nation that is made up of people filled with the Holy Spirit.

One of the great tragedies of the church today is that we are operating on ground level. We are operating like everyone else does—like a civic group or social party. We know the God of the universe and the Creator of the nations, yet we are sitting around waiting for our solutions to land on Air Force One.

If you landed on the moon, you could lift a ton—literally, a ton. But I doubt you would be able to lift a ton on earth. Why can you lift a ton on the moon? Because on the moon you are no longer hindered by gravity.

When you enter another realm, you can handle the weight of things that would have crushed you on earth.

When we survey the many traumas plaguing us as a nation today—not only on a local front, but on a global one—it is easy to throw up our hands, shrug our shoulders, and say that we can't handle the weight of all of this. Yet God has given us a Helper, the Holy Spirit, who can.

DOWN IN THE VALLEY OF BONES

America is not the first nation to be in a situation of seeming hopelessness on a number of levels. In the book of Ezekiel, we get a peek into a time in Israel's history where their dreams had become listless, close to death. They were numb, nearly lifeless.

God's message through his prophet came during the period known as the Babylonian exile. Among the first wave of Judean captives by the Babylonians (2 Kings 24:10–16) near 597 BC, was a young man named Ezekiel. Ezekiel and the fellow deportees were forced to live in a dry place for far too long. They didn't see a way out. They may have examined their own nation's history and recalled what had happened to their sister kingdom Israel whose inhabitants were deported over a century earlier: That land ultimately had fallen into ruin and their people lost their identity to such a degree that eventually they became known as the lost tribes of Israel.

Ezekiel and his countrymen suffered loss on many levels as well—the loss of their city, temple, identity, traditions, rituals, and the Davidic monarchy. As a result, a number of people even lost their faith (Psalm 115:2). A major collapse had occurred, and no one offered up any real solutions on how to fix it. Dreams and hopes had been aborted, birthing barrenness in their stead. The countrymen had been lulled into despair and apathy's curse. If there was no way out of such a desperate situation, then why try any longer? Why not just roll over, cover up, and go back to bed?

But that's why God sent His alarm—Ezekiel—and why He sent him a vision of a hopeless valley filled with dry bones. As you know, a valley is a low place. It's that place where you have to look up just to see bottom—where there are no apparent answers to your dilemma as you live life in crisis mode.

We first get a glimpse of Ezekiel's vision in chapter 37 of the book by his name,

> The hand of the Lord was upon me, and He brought me out by the Spirit of the Lord and set me down in the middle of the valley; and it was full of bones. He caused me to pass among them round about, and behold, there were very many on the surface of the valley; and lo, they were very dry. (vv. 1–2)

In order for bones to be dry, they have to have been there awhile. In order for bones to have been there awhile, bodies had to be in the valley for quite some time. So why were these bones there for so long, and what did they represent? We discover the answer in verse 11. "Then He said to me, 'Son of man, these bones are the whole house of Israel; behold, they say, "Our bones are dried up and our hope has perished. We are completely cut off."'" The bones represent the hope of Israel, or lack thereof. By this point in their exile, they had given up. They had thrown in the towel. They could no longer see a way out of the darkness that surrounded them.

The term "completely cut off" also refers to their fellowship with God, which at one point had been intimate, but was now removed. While they had in many ways kept a semblance of religion and rules, they had lost their relationship through their rebellion.

In verse 23 we read about how God desires to undo this rebellion by returning them to Him: "They will no longer defile themselves with their idols, or with their detestable things, or with any of their transgressions; but I will deliver them from all their dwelling places in which they have sinned, and will cleanse them. And they will be My people, and I will be their God."

This lays out the vision of God's ultimate plan, but at the time that Ezekiel stood in the midst of the valley of dry bones, the nation had been cut off due to their decision to replace the one true God with other gods, or to bring other gods alongside of Him, therefore diminishing His impact in their lives. Their sin had worked itself out in their society because now they had been taken captive and lived as exiles in Babylon.

The situation was so bad that when God asked the prophet Ezekiel if the dry bones he saw could possibly live, the prophet essentially said, "I don't know" (v. 3). They had found themselves in a situation with no solution. Their spiritual disconnection had led to a social catastrophe. Only God knew if this scenario could get turned around. Only God knew if this valley of dead bones could live again.

Far too often in America today we likewise fail to make the connection between our sin and society's circumstances. We fail to recognize that it was greed—plain and simple—that led to the housing collapse of 2008 and the subsequent $700 billion bailout. We fail to recognize that it was also greed that led to the subsidizing of junk food in our nation at nearly $20 billion since 1995,[1] which has expanded America's waistline, raised America's blood pressure, and increased America's doles due to rises in health-related unemployment.[2]

These are just two examples of many, but when we fail to make the connection between the spiritual and the social, we fail to seek the solution that can bring real and lasting impact. We fail to address the spiritual root of the physical mayhem. And so we remain there in a valley of dry bones where no one can truly help anyone else out at all.

This is because when your entire nation is comprised of dry bones, each person is as messed up as the other. It's hard to give hope when you don't have hope yourself. It's equally hard to give help when you are helpless.

That's the problem related to so much of what we're struggling with in our country today. It's hard to give a lasting bailout if the whole nation needs a bailout in some form or another. We need a bailout on morality, education, community development, personal responsibility, drugs, crime, family stability, economics, health, and more. We need a bailout in so many arenas, and yet those best positioned to provide a spiritual bailout, the body of Christ, are facing their own sets of valleys themselves. We have divided over class, culture, and denominations. We lose thousands of pastors due to immorality or burnout. And we have softened our seats instead of rolled up our sleeves.

I find it alarming that in America we have more Christian books than you could ever read, more Christian radio than you could ever listen to, more Christian social media sites than you could ever visit, yet we are a nation of dry bones. We are a nation in a deep valley.

The reason why this is so is because an authentic spiritual life doesn't come about through rituals, budgets, programs, buildings, or even religion. Spiritual life, power, and strength come from the Spirit. The closer we are to the Spirit, the more abundant life we experience. The farther we are from the Spirit, the more decay and death we experience.

DANCE—DRY BONES, DANCE!

Our spiritual situation in America has led to our social disintegration. We have dry people contributing to dry families attending dry churches while living in a dry nation. And as Ezekiel said in verse 3, only God knows how to get those dry bones to dance again. God gave Ezekiel a two-part plan to get those bones to dance again, which included both His Word and His Spirit.

In verse 4 we read, "Prophecy over these bones and say to them, 'O dry bones, hear the word of the Lord.'" Basically, God told Ezekiel to speak His word into their dead situation. God didn't want Ezekiel to tell them what he thought, or to give human ideas and opinions. He didn't ask Ezekiel to give them the popular viewpoint of the day, to cater to their emotional well-being, provide a psychological analysis, or take a Gallup poll. He didn't ask Ezekiel to tell them something designed to make them feel good. God asked Ezekiel to give the dry bones His Word because now that they had reached the point of personal, familial, and national inabilities, God knew that they would listen.

After His Word, He gave them His Spirit. We read, "Thus says the Lord God to these bones, 'Behold, I will cause breath to enter you that you may come to life'" (Ezekiel 37:5). The original word translated as "breath" in this verse is the identical word God used to identify His Spirit referring to the creation process in Genesis 1:2. With His Spirit, God breathed new life into the dead bones. Through this combination of both the Word of God along with His Spirit, God brought about the start of revival in the land.

Our nation is poised for revival. We have reached the end of ourselves.

This is because one of the roles of the Holy Spirit is to take the Word of God and make it come alive in our lives. Like a copier that takes a picture of a written document and copies it onto another piece of paper, the Holy Spirit takes God's Word and transfers its truth into our experiences. In verses 7–10 of Ezekiel, we read about this movement of a very literal revival:

> So I prophesied as I was commanded; and as I prophesied, there was a noise, and behold, a rattling; and the bones came together, bone to its bone. And I looked, and behold, sinews were on them, and flesh grew and skin covered them.... And the breath came into them, and they came to life and stood on their feet, an exceedingly great army.

How long had the bones been in the valley Ezekiel walked? Years. The nation had been out of God's will for a very long time. But God can turn stuff around on a dime when it's time.

Our nation is poised for revival. We have reached the end of ourselves—that place where we realize that we cannot solve nor resurrect the death around us on our own. We are similar to a car battery that has died, and unless someone else comes with jumper cables to connect the two batteries and attach it to the running engine, we will remain dead.

The only way that battery will get recharged is through the transference of life from another. The only way our nation will experience revival is through connecting to God's Spirit.

A valley of dry bones is the last place anyone would look for "an exceedingly great army" (v. 10). After all, it's hard to be a solider and go out to fight to save someone else when you can't even save yourself. Yet from this scattered and dead mess, God rose up an army to advance His cause and bring life to others in the land.

Stuff that had lain there rotting and dead, disassociated with one another—like puzzle pieces in a box—began to connect on their own and soon became the living portrait of a vast army. The Word of God put the pieces together in order to connect bone with bone, muscle with muscle, and sinew with sinew. Likewise, God's Word orders our own lives when we read and apply it. When families live in alignment with His teachings, and churches function in alignment with His precepts, the nation feels its effect. When individuals, businesses, politicians all align with God and His Word, there is order. When that alignment connects with the breath of God's Spirit, there is life from death—a resuscitation occurs.

In biology, we would call that a revival.

In theology, we call it the same.

SEEKING THE SPIRIT

If we want to employ the Spirit's power in our lives and in our land, we will need to make His passion our priority. What is the Holy Spirit's passion? We see it repeatedly in Scripture. Jesus said it best in John 16:13–14: "He will not speak on His own initiative. . . . He will glorify Me, for He will take of Mine, and will disclose it to you." The Spirit's passion is to glorify the Son, Jesus Christ. In the mysterious and wonderful inner workings of the Trinity, it was determined that the Spirit would come to magnify Jesus Christ. Therefore, if Jesus Christ is a low priority in your life, then you will be a low priority in the Spirit's work. I'm not saying the Spirit will quit convicting and drawing you, and He certainly won't stop loving or indwelling you. But don't expect to enjoy the benefits of the Spirit if your commitment to Christ is anemic.

So is loving and serving Christ your driving passion? Is glorifying Him, reflected by obedience to His Word, what gets you up in the morning and keeps you going all day? If it is, you won't have to hunt for the Spirit. He has already tracked you down.

In John 7:37–39, Jesus promises that those who believe on Him will experience "rivers of living water" flowing from their "innermost being" (v. 38). John then tells that Jesus was talking about the Holy Spirit (v. 39), who would come on the day of Pentecost to indwell and energize believers. The same water that is to flow from God's temple as we saw in an earlier chapter and thus heal the landscape of the land, is the same water available to flow from you and from all of us corporately. Jesus' description of the Spirit's presence is that of "living water." The Holy Spirit is a life-giving Spirit.

When He dominates your life, He will make you more alive than you ever thought you could be. You will not only be fulfilled yourself, but the river of living water flowing out of you will overflow so others can be positively influenced by your life as well.

One reason we have so little spiritual power in the church of Jesus Christ today is that we are not thirsty Christians. God only satisfies those who are thirsty. If you are not thirsty, you don't get to drink. What we need is to develop our spiritual thirst. We need a generation of Christians who are passionate for Christ. Unless that is your goal, studying the Bible is a waste of time; coming to church will make little or no difference in your life. The life-giving, thirst-quenching fellowship of the Holy Spirit is enjoyed where the passion of Jesus Christ, and the glory of His name and obedience to His Word, is sought above all.

God only satisfies those who are thirsty. We need to develop our spiritual thirst.

When Jesus Christ is our collective passion as His body—when we do as the young girl, Florrie Evans, did so boldly when she stood to proclaim, "I love Jesus Christ—with all my heart"—thus beginning the 1904 Welsh Revival, God will respond with both the manifest presence and the impactful power of His Holy Spirit. He will ignite the fire and fan the flame of revival in our land.

PART 3

Turning a Nation

9

The Danger of Independence

Every July 4 Americans experience a grand festival. Most of us will spend our time with family and friends enjoying fireworks, barbecue, parades, and more in celebration of Independence Day. We mark that day in 1776 when representatives from the thirteen colonies in America issued a declaration that they would no longer operate underneath the rule of King George III of England.

By right of this declaration, these colonies would cease being under subjection to the parliament of Britain. That kingdom would no longer own nor dominate the people of this land. The signers of the Declaration of Independence thus established the United States of America.

As you know, representatives of the thirteen colonies signed the Declaration of Independence one year after the Revolutionary War began. The signees were branded traitors. And in "declaring themselves an independent nation, the American colonists were able to conclude an official alliance with the government of France and obtain French assistance in the war."[1]

MANKIND'S DECLARATION OF INDEPENDENCE

Why did the Revolutionary War began? Because rebellion always leads to conflict. The signing of the Declaration was the ultimate rebellion, committed to paper.

While it is one thing for colonies to rebel from another nation with unjust oppression, taxation, and structures, it is an entirely different thing for mankind to rebel against the one true God in a desire for independence. Yet that is exactly what we have done and are doing in our nation today. Across the land we have issued a declaration of independence from God Himself. However, independence from God does not lead to freedom at all; rather, it leads to bondage by the ruling forces of another kingdom operated by the darkness of this world.

There are two spiritual kingdoms in existence—God's and Satan's. Good and evil. Right and wrong. Independence from God and His attributes, protection, covenant, and grace equates to dependence on Satan and his chaos, consequences, and calamity.

God is the ultimate ruler of our world. He is the rightful and just King over all. To seek independence from Him is to invite mayhem, which is what has been done both on a personal and national level in our land.

A WRONG DIAGNOSIS

Much of what we witness today in American culture has been misdiagnosed by members of our news media. News analysts often give a political diagnosis for what has gone wrong, or an economic one, or even a social diagnosis. Yet what is happening in our land today and what is happening in our lives is spiritual at its root and must be diagnosed spiritually. The right diagnosis is personal and corporate rebellion against our maker.

The Bible gives us a clear picture of what happens to a nation who seeks to issue a Declaration of Independence from God in the story found in Genesis 11. We are introduced to this epic drama with these words: "Now the whole earth used the same language and the same words." By this we understand that the people of that day had the greatest opportunity for unity ever. There was no division of discourse. Likely, as a result, there was little division of culture. They shared a common confession of agreement. Basically, the whole earth was on the same page.

With this unity, they decided to travel east. To travel east up until this point in Scripture meant to go away from God. This began with Cain when Cain rebelled against God and went east (Genesis 4:16). Thus our story unfolds with a unified nation wanting to leave God's authority.

In other words, they wanted to be one nation away from God rather than one nation under God. So they came up with a plan which we read about in Genesis. "Come, let us build for ourselves a city, and a tower whose top will reach into heaven, and let us make for ourselves a name" (Genesis 11:4).

"LET US"

They began by mirroring God—"Come, let us." After all, it was God who first said, "Let us" when He chose to make mankind in His own image (Genesis 1:26). Now, in our story, we see that very mankind seeking to "Come, let us" themselves. They wanted to come up with their own plan for how life was to be lived and society would be advanced. We know this because of the latter part of verse 4 which says, ". . . otherwise we will be scattered abroad over the face of the whole earth." They wanted to establish a city, build a tower, and make a name for themselves so that they wouldn't have to do what God had asked them to do.

To scatter abroad had been God's plan all along. He first gave His plan to Adam and Eve in which they were to be fruitful and multiply and fill the earth. He later gave the same command to Noah and his sons (Genesis 9:1.) Now the creation wanted to rebel from that command. They wanted to establish their own base from which to operate so that they could remain in one place.

In order to do this they sought to use the technology of the day—bricks and mortar—to construct a tower. They chose to develop their own ingenious way of formulating civilization and a world system, not realizing that their technology had ignored God's creation. Technology will do that. It will draw a person or society away from God rather than to Him, the source of all things.

The further we have advanced technologically in our nation, the more independent from God we have become. When we can create things in a masterful way that highlights the brilliance and intelligence of man, we lose the felt need for God. And so the people went east from His presence with their bricks and mortar, believing they could construct a world of their own.

THE CREATOR–CREATURE DISTINCTION

The people of Babel wanted to be the source of their own meaning, the definition of their own existence. Through willful defiance, they sought to erase the Creator–creature distinction. In theological terms, we use the large word "transcendence" to mean, among other things, that God sits outside of His creation and is not to be confused with it. He sits above and beyond it and is not the same as it. While He works within it, He is distinct from it. To seek to remove that distinction is to seek to become your own god.

If you are a parent of a teenager, or have been a parent of a teenager, then you probably know this firsthand. Often, as was the case of the teenagers living in my home, they want to be independent while still living in your house. They don't want you telling them what to do, giving them instructions or expectations. Yet they do want you to pay the mortgage, put gas in the car, buy their food, and keep them comfortable with air-conditioning or heat. Essentially, they want independence while depending. We all know that it doesn't work that way.

We depend on God for more things than we even realize. Not only does He supply the ability for life itself, He has created our very lives and gives us the essentials to continue living. He supplies the food, rain, warmth, intelligence, natural resources, oxygen—everything. There is no such thing, then, as independence from God on earth. For anyone. Rather, there is only a seeking of independence while depending. Which, as it does in any home with a teenager seeking to do the same, produces conflict and consequences.

GOD CAME DOWN

The people building the tower of Babel sought to do three things: Create a city, build a tower to the heavens, and make a name for themselves. The city would serve as a centralized location of government. The tower, stretching to the heavens, would serve as a religious symbol of equality, replacing theocracy with self-rule. Their own man-made religion would give them religious justification for their rebellion. Making a name for themselves would serve as an identification of independence, sovereignty, and power apart from God. They wanted to define themselves by themselves and become the source of their own meaning. Reason would then replace revelation. When men refuse to be ruled by God, then they will seek to emulate Him.

However, what they forgot in this process is that no matter how high mankind can rise, God still has to come down to reach him. Genesis 11:5 reads, "The Lord came down to see the city and the tower which the sons of men had built."

No matter how big a country's name is, no matter how much

money it has, no matter how much influence it wields or how high it can climb, God is transcendent. He sits not only above but also beyond Earth. He must come down in order to reach it because He is larger than the sum total of His creation.

What God unearthed when He came down, though, and what we discover in studying this incident in history is one of the most powerful tools we can use in turning a nation to God. We read, "The Lord said, 'Behold, they are one people, and they all have the same language. And this is what they began to do, and now nothing which they purpose to do will be impossible for them'" (v. 6).

In this one verse we find one of the greatest principles for advancing God's kingdom on earth in the entire Bible: oneness. God had already given humanity the Dominion Covenant (Genesis 1:26–28) when He said "let them rule." God would recognize the decisions of mankind in history. This coupled with unity left no limitation. Thus God addresses the power of oneness when He acknowledges in His Word that the people who shared a common language, vision, and goal—and set their minds to accomplish it—would find nothing impossible before them. In other words, God affirms there is power in unity even when that unity is against Him.

THE POWER OF ONENESS

God's response to this reality was swift and final. He determined to scramble their language, thus causing confusion, and to scatter their proximity (Genesis 11:7–8) thus forcing them to obey His earlier commands to fill the earth. Division and separation make impotent mankind's attempts at progress and change. God used it for His purposes at the Tower of Babel, and Satan uses the same tactic for his purposes in disunifying the body of Christ. This is because unity brings with it many benefits, of which the power to accomplishing things is just one.

Another aspect of power in oneness is the ability to glorify God.

This is because oneness reflects His image through His triune nature. And when we glorify God, God gets behind what we do. In those times where He is truly being made known to the world in all of His glory, the power of His backing and covering is there. The importance of this truth comes through clearly in Jesus' prayer, commonly referred to as Jesus' high priestly prayer, shortly before He was arrested and crucified. He prayed,

> I pray also for those who will believe in me through their message, that all of them may be *one*, Father, just as you are in me and I am in you. May they also be in us so that the world may believe that you have sent me. I have given them the glory that you gave me, that they may be *one* as we are *one*—I in them and you in me— so that they may be brought to *complete unity*. Then the world will know that you sent me and have loved them even as you have loved me. (John 17:20–23 NIV, italics added)

Jesus Christ placed a tremendous emphasis on His desire for us to be one as His followers just hours before He would lay down His life for us. This isn't something that He is asking us to do only once in a while, either. This is a mandate from our Commander in Chief that we be *one* with Him (vertically) and, as a result, *one* with each other (horizontally) and thus expand His kingdom on the earth.

Oneness also increases our power to promote positive change by moving us into the atmosphere where we can experience God's response as He manifests His glory most fully. The fullest possible manifestation of God's presence functions in a spirit of oneness in the body of Christ. This is precisely why the subject found its place as the core of Jesus' high priestly prayer. It was the core because it uniquely reveals God's Trinitarian nature unlike anything else. It does this while at the same time revealing an authentic connection among those in the body of Christ, which serves as a testimony of our connection with Christ.

Unity is where the blessing of God rests, coming down from heaven to flow from the head to the body.

Jesus says, "By this all men will know that you are My disciples, if you have love for one another" (John 13:35).

An additional benefit of oneness is found in the Old Testament passage penned by David: "Behold, how good and how pleasant it is for brothers to dwell together in unity! It is like the precious oil upon the head, coming down upon the beard, even Aaron's beard, coming down upon the edge of his robes. It is like the dew of Hermon coming down upon the mountains of Zion; for there the Lord commanded the blessing—life forever" (Psalm 133:1–3).

Unity is where the blessing of God rests, coming down from heaven to flow from the head to the body, and even reaching as far as the mountains of Zion. In other words, it covers everything. Unity is the only condition in Scripture where God commands a blessing.

The reverse is also true: Where there is disunity, there is limited blessing. We cannot operate in disunity and expect the full manifestation and continuation of God's blessing in our lives. We cannot operate in disunity and expect to hear from heaven, or expect God to answer our prayers in the way that both we and He longs for Him to do. Disunity—or an existence of separatism, from a spiritual perspective—is essentially at its core self-defeating and self-limiting because it reduces the movement of God's favor and blessings.

Jesus made it clear that a house divided against itself cannot stand. Whether it is your house, the church house, or the White House—division leads to destruction (Matthew 12:25). Yet a house united can change the landscape of the entire world. Just take a look at the beginning of the global church in Acts 2 where we see the manifestation of the Holy Spirit who was moving like a "violent rushing wind" and "filled the whole house where they were sitting" (Acts 2:2), in the midst of the oneness of the believers on the Day of Pentecost.

At the end of the second chapter, the presence and product of oneness is emphasized as we read, "Everyone kept feeling a sense of awe; and many wonders and signs were taking place through the apostles. And all those who had believed were together and had all things in common" (Acts 2:43–44). Signs and wonders took place when they were "together" and "had all things in common." God manifested Himself when they were one.

When they were one, God poured His blessing from heaven into history.

What made this place and this period in time so electric was that the Spirit of God had taken over. The miracles taking place did not happen because the individuals had the best program, the best technology, or the biggest buildings in which to meet. They didn't have any of that. In fact, they barely had any income. Among the people no one had fame, academic success, or charisma. They were simply common people bonded together by a common purpose across racial, class, and gender lines, thus receiving the Spirit's flow among them. Their unity garnered both power and influence.

When they were one, God poured His blessing from heaven into history. God chose to do things that He would not otherwise have done if His people had not been one.

Conversely, remaining in an environment of intellectual, spiritual, or denominational separatism limits the involvement of God's blessings in our personal lives, families, churches, and communities and as a result, limits our impact on society.

Keep in mind, oneness is not just about racial unity. That is often the first thing we will think of when talking about this subject. But the dividing lines in the body of Christ within the United States have less to do with race than they do with many other things. We are also divided by denomination, location, class, politics, vision, and the like. As I said earlier, we have more churches and more nonprofit parachurch organizations than ever before—yet we are having less cultural influence than ever before.

One of the reasons I believe this is so is because we are each seeking to construct our own Tower of Babel—our own names, growth, prominence, and platform rather than aligning together under the one name of Jesus Christ and having a collective and impactful platform never witnessed nor experienced before.

Should we maintain a variety of churches and denominations? Yes. Should we maintain multiple parachurch and mission organizations? Yes. I'm not recommending that we create one centralized religious entity over them all similar to the Roman Catholic Church. But I am suggesting that we set our own agendas to the side for those strategic times when a collective voice would be the wisest and most powerful voice of all.

And I believe that this collective voice is needed now in our nation. It is needed now for us to carry out a national solemn assembly with the hopes of ushering in a national revival bringing lasting cultural transformation and change.

God knows the power of unity. He knows it so well that when the unregenerate sought to make a name for themselves by uniting in the building of the Tower of Babel, God's response was to disunify them. Likewise, He has given us the high calling of being one with Him and with each other because He knows that in our unity we will access His manifest presence and power.

OUR LOST INFLUENCE

One of the great tragedies in the church of Jesus Christ today is that we have lost our ability and authority to influence those around us. We have lost this because we have divided and aligned ourselves with the power and preferences of man. We have let the compromising realities of politics erect a division between us, permitting political expedience to override the kingdom of God.

Until we recognize each other as representatives of the same kingdom, thus responding through an intentional embracing of oneness in purpose, we will continue to contribute to the devolution of our land. We will fill the airwaves of society's conscience with a cacophony of chaos rather than with the liberating cadence of truth.

God has not given His allegiance to any political party or agenda. His allegiance belongs to Himself—His Word and His kingdom.

Think of the impact we could have as the body of Christ if we would seek to advance God's agenda in a unified fashion. Simply defined, *biblical unity is oneness of purpose.* Unity is not uniformity. Unity means moving together toward the same goal. If every player on a football team was a running back, the team wouldn't accomplish their goal of scoring touchdowns. Likewise, God created each of us unique with unique strengths and abilities. By merging these strengths and abilities together toward a common purpose, we live out true unity and experience its effects.

The clearest example of the opposite of this was given to me by Billy Graham when I was spending some time with him at his home one afternoon. In his typical dignified way, Dr. Graham leaned toward me in his chair and voiced his frustrations on how churches would come together for the sake of evangelism but then go back to their own disconnected corners after his event had ended. If these churches were kingdom-minded, he postulated, their collective impact in the community would have been ongoing.

Unfortunately, we've allowed the separation in politics, power, and preferences to create a separation in the church as well. Because of that, we are making little visible difference in the culture at large.

Instead of sharing a like voice toward a like goal, churches often try to reinvent the wheel in terms of their agenda and strategy, leaving only a mere dent in society rather than true transformation. Rarely, if ever, have we joined together toward a shared purpose or vision. Because of this, we lack the collective impact we ought to be having on our land.

OUR LOST DEFENSE

Not only are we lacking in our impact, but we are also lacking in our defense, as Satan is wreaking havoc all across America. He's not only fortifying the ground he has already taken; he's grabbing new ground every day. Through our disobedience and disunity, Christ's church unintentionally is aiding the decline of our nation. This brings about God's passive wrath—when He allows a society to experience the natural negative consequences of its rebellion (Romans 1:18–32).

The apostle Peter says that Satan is a roaring lion, seeking whom he may devour (1 Peter 5:8). The problem is that many Christians don't know when lions roar. Lions do not roar when they are getting ready to kill their prey; they roar after they kill their prey. Why? Because lions want to chase away the hyenas.

Hyenas are scavengers that travel in packs, eating the carcasses of dead animals. Because the lions know they cannot defeat a pack of jackals working together, they roar in order to intimidate them from advancing toward the prey. The hyenas get so intimidated by the roars that they forget the power of their unity. Rather than advancing, they retreat.

Satan is like the lions. He has a big mouth, but if the church would just keep on coming, our collective power would easily drive him from his control of the carcasses of our decaying communities, cities, and nation.

Friends and fellow believers, if we truly want to turn our nation to God, we must first—as the body of Christ—return to Him ourselves. Secondly, and just as importantly, we must turn toward each other in a spirit of oneness. And then, together, issue a new Declaration—this time a Declaration of Dependence on our God and King.

10

The Partnership of Church and State

America is quickly becoming a far different nation than it ever was before. The root of the problem facing us, though, keenly reflects what the prophet Ezekiel spoke of concerning the Israelites in his day. In that day for Israel, like today for America, the people no longer comprised "one nation under God."

The prophet's words, found in Ezekiel 43, addressed the return of the glory of God to the temple. God's previous absence had brought chaos in the land. The citizens witnessed an increase in crime, social deterioration, and a lack of order.

Now in announcing God's return, Ezekiel quotes God's reasons for leaving a wayward people. Ezekiel writes:

He [God] said to me, "Son of man, this is the place of My throne and the place of the soles of My feet, where I will dwell among the sons of Israel forever. And the house of Israel will not again defile My holy name, neither they nor their kings, by their harlotry and by the corpses of their kings when they die, by setting their threshold by My threshold and their door post beside My door post, with only the wall between Me and them. And they have defiled My holy name by their abominations which they have committed. So I have consumed them in My anger. Now let them put away their harlotry and the corpses of their kings far from Me; and I will dwell among them forever." (Ezekiel 43:7–9)

God said that the human kings (the government) had been allowed to put their throne next to His throne in His house. They therefore intruded their rule on His own. Erecting a partition to divide the two, the governments of man set up shop among God's rule in God's house.

God had made it inextricably clear that His house was to have only one throne—His own. But Israel had allowed politics to interfere with God's house. Or in our day, they had allowed classism, partisan politics, racism, secularism, humanism, and the like to intrude on His viewpoint and His rule—in His house.

Because of that, God's glory left. God's covering departed. His influence, power, protection, and guidance was removed because Israel invited another throne to sit next to His own.

God created the church to act as a vehicle for His rule and glory. It is not the Democrats' view *and* God's view that we are to proclaim in the church. Neither is it the Republicans' view *and* God's view that we are to have. It is only God who rules.

PARTISAN POLITICS VERSUS GOD'S KINGDOM

Yet the problem today is that far too many churches have been corrupted by civil religion. They have failed to recognize the difference between partisan politics and God's kingdom. This plays out in more ways than simply politics, though. It plays out in bringing the world's values into God's house and raising them up to receive the same level of adherence and attention as God, if not more.

Because the church has lost its own conscience in many ways, it has failed in its calling to be a conscience for society, not only through the civic participation of its members, but likewise through their own daily governance in their personal lives and families. We have allowed what the society gives us in our media, schools, policies, and philosophies to infiltrate and infect the church.

The church is to be the key to the transformation of the culture, not the other way around. In the past, the church effectively influenced the society in many ways. In fact, it was because of the emphasis of the freedom of religion, as promoted by the body of Christ, that America was born. It was also because of the promotion of freedom and equality for all, in large part through the church, that civil rights for African-Americans was achieved. In both cases, the church went against the grain of what was commonly accepted in the culture.

The body of Christ is not a democracy to be influenced by the opinions of the majority. The church is God's legislative agency in history to be governed by His Word in order to reflect and promote that governance in every area of life.

Many people want "God bless America" today. They don't want "One nation under God."

Many people want "God bless America" today. They just don't want "One nation under God." The issue is that you can't have one without the other. But it's hard to strive for one nation under God when we can't even get one church under God.

God has given us the freedom to choose whether we will be one under Him—whether we will recognize His rule and operate underneath it. But with that choice comes either "God bless America" or not. God only promises to bless the people who recognize His authority (Psalm 33:12). And while America was never officially a Christian nation since neither Jesus Christ nor the Bible are referenced in the Constitution or the Declaration of Independence, its dominant influence throughout its inception was the Christian faith because of the voice of the churches and Christian laity in the land.

We are a nation of freedom. And even God has given us freedom. However, freedom only means you get to control the choice. But because God is the sovereign ruler over His creation—you don't get to control the consequences. He will rule by either endorsing your choice, or He will rule by allowing you to have the consequences of a decision made against Him.

ALL THINGS TO ALL PEOPLE

We read in Psalm 103 that, "The Lord has established His throne in the heavens, and His sovereignty rules over all" (v:19). In Daniel, it says that "the Most High is ruler over the realm of mankind" (Daniel 4:17), and that "it is Heaven that rules" (Daniel 4:26).

Scripture clearly distinguishes for us in these places and in many others that God's rule operates universally over everything, every nation, person, and system, whether that be political, economic, educational, or familial. Yet while there is one ultimate Ruler, there are multiple rulers who have been put in place in order to rule. That is why Paul tells us to be in subjection to the governing authorities (Romans 13:1).

The reason for the plurality in governing authorities is because the division of power provides the best environment for the fair disbursement of power underneath the ultimate ruler, God. Just like at the Tower of Babel when mankind tried to unite in order to usurp or reach God's rulership in the heavens, God resisted their attempt at a centralized world power (Genesis 11:1–9).

It is in dividing up governing authorities that both checks and balances are put in place against such evils arising within a sinful humanity such as tyranny and dictatorships. That is why our founding fathers separated the judicial from the legislative and also from the executive branches of government. Since God exists as both unity and diversity

(Trinity), human government has been established to reflect that pattern by being unified in their purpose while being diversified in their spheres of responsibility.

The division of power is the biblical and most optimal way for maximizing God's position as the ultimate authority. Government cannot be all things to all people. Only God can be everything for the people. When the State seeks to adopt such a role, it is seeking to emulate God.

Civil government is to support, not replace, the other two institutions of government (family and church).

It is true that civil government is that system which has been set in place to create and maintain a righteous, safe, and just environment in which freedom can flourish. It is a representative system designed to manage society in an orderly fashion. Yet it is to do so without interfering with, negating, or contradicting God's other governing agencies. Civil government is to support, not replace, the other two institutions of government (family and church) so that self-government, and therefore maximum freedom, can be experienced. It is not to dictate the purposes or precepts of the church.

Paul emphasizes the primary existence of civil government in the continuation of his discussion in Romans 13 when he writes, "Therefore whoever resists authority has opposed the ordinance of God; and they who have opposed will receive condemnation upon themselves. For rulers are not a cause of fear for good behavior, but for evil" (vv. 2–3).

In these verses, Paul introduces us to the one overarching job of civil government, which can be defined as this: *Under God, civil government is to promote the conditions for the well-being of the citizenry for good while protecting the citizenry against the proliferation of evil.* Since civil government is to operate under God, He—and not man—must be the ultimate standard of what is good or evil. This means that politics is fundamentally an ethical enterprise based on what is right and what is wrong as God defines it.

When civil government successfully keeps evil in check, good can flourish. This holds true whether that means keeping the evil out that shows up in our enemies around the world, or whether that means keeping people from knocking down your front door. Government is to restrict the flow of evil while simultaneously and intentionally seeking to expand the flow of good. Everything within civil government ought to be aimed at this one primary goal.

Paul explains:

> Do you want to have no fear of authority? Do what is good and you will have praise from the same; *for it is a minister of God to you for good.* But if you do what is evil, be afraid; for it does not bear the sword for nothing; for it is a minister of God, *an avenger who brings wrath on the one who practices evil.* (Romans 13:3–4, italics added)

When civil government attempts to do more than that, it typically ends up infringing on other divinely authorized governments (individual, family, and/or church). When the government tries to act as someone's parent and pay someone's bills while they do not work, the government has become more than the government was designed to be. The Bible says if a man does not work, he ought not to eat (2 Thessalonians 3:10). It is not talking about when a man cannot work. It is talking about when a man won't work. If a man does not work, you do not offer him a welfare check to pay him for his irresponsibility. You don't look to the government to pay for laziness while taxing others to cover the bill.

Just as God restricts the church from giving charity to people prior to getting the family involved first (1 Timothy 5:4), civil government is not to provide charity prior to the involvement of the family, church, and other local charitable entities. Help is to be given by those closest related to the need who can provide both love and accountability that promotes personal freedom and responsibility.

What government can do in making this happen is to create an environment for compassion to flourish—similar to its protection and encouragement of faith-based initiatives in the early 2000s. That falls under its task to promote good. When this order is reversed—as it has been a few years ago—then the state becomes an all-encompassing promoter of federal economic dependency, leading to illegitimate and irresponsible personal and corporate welfare.

Limited government, however, does not mean uncaring and uncompassionate government. Civil government should provide a safety net for those responsible people who fall through the cracks of God's other governmental entities. Such government assistance for able-bodied citizens should be temporary and not designed to produce long-term dependency and an entitlement mentality. Government assistance should always be accompanied with accountability for demonstrating responsibility through various means, such as developing an employable skill or volunteerism.

When civil government is limited to its primary role, while maintaining an environment for God's other governments to flourish, it does not overextend itself and those underneath it while trying to be everything to everybody while still charging taxpayers for things it does not have divine authorization to do. An overextended civil government and overtaxed citizenry limits the freedoms of individuals to pursue their calling under God, and their capacity to contribute to economic development. It also creates an environment of restriction, doubt, and concern, thus stifling both opportunity and ingenuity.

A limited civil government is not one that excludes the priority of justice functioning in society. On the contrary, it promotes it. What it does do is free up the other governments to fulfill their responsibility without being illegitimately infringed upon.

The problem comes when civil government tries to be more than it was designed to be, or fails to protect or promote that which government was designed to protect or promote. When civil government expands and reaches into the other three spheres of government God has instituted (individual, family, and church), tyranny results reflected in high taxation and subsequently causing civil government to grow far beyond its divinely authorized scope—allowing it to both confiscate and redistribute that which is not lawfully theirs, as was in the case of 1 Samuel 8:10–18.

The economic responsibility of civil government is to remove fraud and coercion from the marketplace, thus keeping it free from tyranny. It is not to control the marketplace. At best, it should seek to compete in the marketplace demonstrating its ability to function efficiently, effectively, and for a profit rather than control the marketplace because of its size, power, or ability to print money.

Centralized governmental control of trade is the economic system of the Antichrist (Revelation 13:17). This means that the centralized governmental ownership or control of the ways and means of production is against God (i.e. socialism and communism).

IN THE BEGINNING, GOD WAS THE GOVERNMENT

In the beginning, God was the government. His model allowed for broad freedom along with narrow restrictions, followed up with both quick and severe consequences for breaking those restrictions. Yet after the fall of mankind, God transferred the carrying out of the government of mankind to men. God had set the standard for how His creation should operate and then transferred that standard of government to mankind after sin entered the world.

Therefore a government patterned after the original design of the Creator is a government that does not seek to limit humanity's freedoms, but rather promotes freedom through the declaration of clear and just boundaries along with the carrying out of immediate and acute consequences for breaking those boundaries. It is in this type of government where individuals, families, churches, and local communities are best equipped to cultivate and maintain high levels of both productivity and enjoyment so that free enterprise can flourish.

Freedom is so important that we must be involved not only in fighting for it for ourselves, but also in empowering others to experience it as well. This is why the greatest demonstration of our value and appreciation for freedom is realized in diligently serving the well-being of others (Galatians 5:13). Freedom's purest form is manifested through expanding and enriching the freedom of others.

Civil government exists, therefore, to promote personal and collective freedom through resisting evil and overseeing the proliferation of good through maintaining a just and righteous society. When a government fails to do this either because it runs inefficiently or ineffectively—fundamentally unjustly or unrighteously—it is typically the masses who suffer.

THE PARTNERSHIP OF CHURCH AND STATE

The Bible has a lot to say on the political realm. In fact, it is thick with politics. Two books, 1 and 2 Kings, recount the reigns of government leaders. The New Testament accounts several instances of political intrigue. John the Baptist condemned the immoral conduct of Herod Antipas, and the prophet's execution ensued (Mark 6:14–29). In Thessalonica, Paul and his companions were charged with committing treason against Rome for insisting "that there is another king, Jesus" (Acts 17:7). Revelation tells us that in the greatest act of political and moral rebellion ever against God, the Antichrist one day will set up his worldwide government of pure evil, and he will rule the earth (Revelation 13:1–10).

Because God is the Sovereign of His universe, it follows that He is intimately concerned with the political affairs of the nations. There is nothing that happens in the governments of men that does not flow out of the sovereign rule of God. "The king's heart is like channels of water in the hand of the Lord; He turns it wherever He wishes" (Proverbs 21:1).

All through the Bible, we see God placing people strategically in the political realm. He moved Joseph into political authority in Egypt (Genesis 41:38–49) and elevated Daniel to a position of great governmental influence in Babylon and later in Persia (Daniel 1:8–21; 2:46–49; 6:1–3). God also placed Nehemiah in the Persian government so he could rebuild his community with government support (Nehemiah 1:1–28). He also placed Esther as queen in Persia[1] and Deborah as judge in Israel to accomplish His agenda (Judges 4–5).

There is no escaping God's political activity. We cannot divide life, putting God on one side and politics on the other.

In fact, the greatest example of God's involvement in the political affairs of a nation is Israel itself, where God established the nation's constitution, legal structure, and laws that were to be the model for other nations to emulate (Deuteronomy 4:5–7). Beyond 1 and 2 Kings, God is active on every page of such Bible histories as 1 and 2 Samuel and 1 and 2 Chronicles, setting up this king, judging that king, and deposing of yet another king.

There is no escaping God's political activity. This means we cannot divide life down the middle, putting God on one side and politics on the other.

Now someone may argue that while God was intimately involved in the governing of Israel, that was because God Himself established Israel as a theocracy. But when it comes to the other nations of the earth, God is not that deeply involved. Scripture would not agree with that, because in Daniel 4 we see God getting very personally and intimately involved in the life of King Nebuchadnezzar of Babylon, the greatest secular ruler in the greatest pagan kingdom of the day.

God protested the unrighteousness of Nebuchadnezzar's government because Nebuchadnezzar sought to usurp the authority that belongs to God, which is the sin of every centralized government. In the end, Nebuchadnezzar wound up making the very confession God decreed he would make (vv. 34–37). The farther a government drifts from God (which means it seeks to become its own god), the more it sets itself up for heavenly political action.

And while Israel was a theocracy functioning under biblical law and America is a constitutional republic, the principles of the character of God and its effects on our society come to bear on our culture and must be applied. This is because the Bible says that "by [Jesus] all things were created . . . whether thrones or dominions or rulers or authorities" (Colossians 1:16). And He not only created heavenly and earthly kingdoms (v. 16), they are dependent on Him to "hold together" (v. 17) all things.

The greatest political statement in the Bible is the declaration of Revelation 19:16 that when Jesus Christ returns to earth to rule, He will come as "King of kings, and Lord of lords." Earlier in Revelation 1:5, John had seen a vision of the glorified Jesus, who was declared to be "the ruler of the kings of the earth."

To talk about the activity of God the Father and God the Son both in history and in the future is to merge the sacred with the secular in the arena of politics.

WHAT ABOUT THE SEPARATION
OF CHURCH AND STATE?

While the phrase "separation of church and state" does not appear in our Constitution, many people believe that it does. Yet the First Amendment states "Congress shall make no law respecting an establishment of religion, or prohibiting the free exercise thereof . . ."

The original intent, as outlined by Thomas Jefferson in his letter to the Danbury Baptist Association in 1802 in which the phrase "separation of church and state" was derived, specifically referred to a separation of government infringing on the rights and freedoms of the religious, and not the other way around.

"The United States ought to use any resource available to better communities, and if faith-based organizations are willing to provide community services with clear secular purposes, they should be encouraged to do so," writes Andrew Small.[2]

Good works that are implemented by religious organizations are in effect the exact same types of activities that are implemented by secular organizations to benefit a community. If independent public or private organizations are encouraged to serve their communities, religious organizations with social service initiatives should be part of the "all hands on deck" as well.

While we need a separation of church and state, there can never be a separation of God and good works.

Critics of faith-based initiatives argue that it is not possible for religious organizations to separate their belief systems from their services. Yet, it is possible to offer social services to those in need without forcing religious beliefs on them. Outreach to the community by the local church does not constitute an infringement of church and state separation. Rather, it allows the church the same freedoms of offering much-needed social services as other organizations.

Today, many seek to illegitimately utilize the state to control, limit, or even silence the church's voice and influence in the public arena under the false interpretation and application of the concept of the separation of church and state. And while there must be the institutional separation of church and state, there can never be a separation of God and good works.

The chief end of man is to glorify God. The chief end of the church is to likewise glorify God through expanding and advancing His kingdom. A major way this is accomplished is through good works because good works bring glory to His name (Matthew 5:16). Thus, when we are about the business of doing good to others—whether that be mentoring in public schools, helping those in need, restoring homes for the elderly, discipling couples in the areas of family and parenting, teaching, training, providing food, comfort, and more—we are about the business of our great God and King.

11

Creating Followers, Not Just Fans

When you see a culture that's deteriorating, look closer and you
will probably see a people of God who have withdrawn from
the culture and turned it over to the unrighteous to rule. Consider
these developments in America:

+ When Christians began to abandon inner-city and urban
  neighborhoods, taking their skills, resources, and moral influence with them, those neighborhoods deteriorated.
+ When Christians left the public school system, moral values
  were systematically erased until they became almost illegal
  to teach.
+ When Christians vacated the media, then a spiritual approach to defining everything we hold dear went with them.
+ When Christians decided they ought to get out of politics,
  then the majority of righteous political decisions left with
  them.

God's people have been called to influence society. Thus the goal and the cornerstone of our activity as followers of the King, that which brings God the most glory, is for us to become His disciples. God's goal is not just personal salvation; that is the introduction to God's goal. His desire is that those who are saved become disciples of Jesus.

Discipleship is that *developmental process that progressively brings Christians from spiritual infancy to spiritual maturity so that they are then able to reproduce the process with someone else.* The singular, overarching goal of a disciple is to bring all of life under the lordship of Jesus Christ, and then help someone else to do the same.

The absence of righteousness in our culture has everything to do with the absence of God's people living as His disciples and thus influencing the culture. It's not that God is lacking people altogether; He has a lot of fans. Every Sunday around the country, our churches are packed with fans of Jesus who are content to remain in the stands rather than advance His kingdom down the field of play. Jesus doesn't need more fans. He needs more followers—committed kingdom disciples making an impact in our culture for Him.

BEING THE SALT OF THE EARTH

In Matthew 5:13–16, Jesus gave the distilled essence of His teaching on the subject of influencing the culture. Let's look at the first portion of His metaphor: "You are the salt of the earth; but if the salt has become tasteless, how can it be made salty again? It is no longer good for anything, except to be thrown out and trampled under foot by men" (v. 13).

Notice that Jesus said we are the salt of the earth, not the salt of the salt shaker. No mother or father buys salt so their family can stare at it in the shaker during dinner. The whole point of salt is to leave the shaker and penetrate the food.

You may say, "Tony, that's so obvious it hardly needs to be mentioned." I'm not so sure. We Christians are often at our best when we're all gathered together in the "salt shaker" at church on Sunday. It's easy to be salt in church because you've got all these other grains of salt around you.

Being salty only in church is like playing basketball by yourself. It's a "can't lose" situation. The test of our salt as Christians is what happens when we hit the decaying culture of the world.

PLUS NO ONE

When Jesus said, "You are the salt of the earth," He put the word *you* in the emphatic position. This phrase could be accurately rendered, "You, and nobody else, are the salt of the earth." It's you and me, the church, plus no one.

Why? Because the people of God are the only ones who have been endowed with the spiritual resources necessary to do God's work God's way.

That means it's not you and the government, for example. Now don't get me wrong. I just said that Christians' withdrawal from the political process has contributed to our problem. What I'm talking about here is the difference between involvement and the attitude that politics is the answer, that somehow our problems will land on Air Force One. Our elected officials are called by God to be servants, but politics is not the salt of the earth.

You can't substitute any other earthly organization or group of people into Jesus' statement and come up with the salt of the earth. When Jesus told His disciples, "You and you alone are the salt of the earth," He meant it.

THE PRESERVING QUALITY OF SALT

Salt was a very important commodity in Jesus' day, even more than it is today. In fact, if you have parents or grandparents who live in the countryside, far from a grocery store, they may still salt down their food. The reason, of course, is that salt is a preservative. It's designed to repel bacteria and preserve food.

That was crucial in Jesus' day because they didn't have refrigeration. Salt was so valuable in the ancient world that it was often traded ounce for ounce with gold. Roman soldiers were paid in salt. In fact, the word *salary* is derived from the concept of paying for work with salt.

If a Roman soldier didn't do his job, he would not get all of his salt. That's where we get the phrase "so-and-so is not worth his salt" if he doesn't do a good day's work.

Many believers need to become worth their salt. We are going to have to live up to Jesus' expectations if this world is going to be preserved from decay. There's no one else around to fill the job description of being the salt of the earth.

LOSING YOUR SALTINESS

Look back at Matthew 5:13. Jesus said, "But if the salt has become tasteless, how can it be made salty again? It is no longer good for anything, except to be thrown out and trampled under foot by men."

This is an interesting phrase because Jesus is not saying that you can have "saltless salt." There is no such thing. Salt is a solid compound. The only thing that makes salt is the chemical compound of sodium and chloride. If you extracted either element, what's left would not be salt. So believers cannot become "unsalt."

But we can become "tasteless" salt, and Jesus' phrase "trampled under foot by men" explains how it can happen. In ancient Israel, the homes had flat roofs. People would go up on the rooftop at night to relax or entertain friends or pray or whatever.

The Israelites held wedding receptions on their rooftops. Kids played on the roofs. So there was a lot of walking around on the roof. And sometimes as a roof got trampled upon, a hole would get punched in the roof and the rain would leak into the house. So they would have to patch the hole.

This was done by mixing the mineral gypsum with water, creating a paste, and then thickening it with salt. The mixture was put on the hole in the roof, and the sun would harden it to form a seal and keep the rain out of the house.

But the salt used this way wasn't good for anything else, because gypsum is bitter. The bitterness of the gypsum would overpower the saltiness of the salt, and the salt would lose its taste. It was good only as a roof sealant to be "trampled under foot."

That's a good description of contemporary Christianity. We've become so mixed up with the "gypsum" of this world's way of thinking and living that people can't taste the Christianity in the culture anymore.

So what is the world doing? Walking on us. The world doesn't take the church seriously. It knows we are no risk to them. Why? Because all we are going to do is cluster in our buildings a couple of times a week and not do much of anything when we leave.

THE LIGHT OF THE WORLD

Now I want to pick up the second of Jesus' metaphors in Matthew 5: "You are the light of the world," He told His disciples (v. 14). The last time I checked, lights have one purpose: to shine. That's all they do. People say, "This world is dark." Well, we can expect the world to be dark. It's supposed to be unclarified in its direction because the world is not the light.

We are the light—and the construction in the original language is the same here as we saw earlier. That is, "you" is in the emphatic position. So guess what? When it comes to giving light, it's Christians like you and me and nobody else.

Jesus likened us to "a city set on a hill [that] cannot be hidden"

(v. 14b). Buildings in biblical days were often made of white limestone, which would reflect the light of the moon. So if you were traveling by night in those days, you would know you were near a city when you saw the reflection.

And since many cities in New Testament days were built on hills, their higher elevation and white limestone made them even more easily visible. God wants our representation of Him to be highly visible and unmistakably clear.

That's why we can't afford to hide our light under a basket (v. 15). It needs to be put up high so the beam can reach as far as possible. There is no room for "secret agent" Christians. We are not to be spiritual CIA covert operatives.

People will publicly announce who they are for in any political season by placing placards in their yards, affixing bumper stickers on their cars, wearing pins on their shirts, among other things. They do this all the while knowing that some people will accept them and some people will reject them. Yet that reality does not stop their advertising or their public alignment with the kingdom of their choice. They are not ashamed to be known for the side they're on.

THE LIGHT THAT SHINES FORTH GOD'S GLORY

What we need are people who are unapologetically Christian. As we saw earlier, Jesus said in Matthew 5:16, "Let your light shine before men in such a way that they may see your good works, and glorify your Father who is in heaven." Glorify means "to show off." It means to make God look good, to display His goodness to the world.

Jesus said the way we glorify God is by our good works. Sinners can do good things like build hospitals and orphanages. They can feed the poor and on and on. But sinners cannot do good works in the biblical sense.

What's the difference between good things and good works? Good works are God's goals achieved God's way for God's glory based on God's Word that benefits people. Paul says in Ephesians 2:10, "We are His workmanship, created in Christ Jesus for good works, which God prepared beforehand so that we would walk in them." Good works are God-created works. They aren't things we make up on our own.

We find God-created good works as we become disciples of His Word: "All Scripture is inspired by God and profitable for teaching, for reproof, for correction, for training in righteousness; so that the man of God may be adequate, equipped *for every good work*" (2 Timothy 3:16–17, italics added). Paul was telling Timothy in this passage that scriptural discipleship equips us to live a life of good works.

What we need are committed Christians who are tired of the status quo and who want to be used of God to turn things around. If not you, who? And if not now, when? Our decaying culture needs the church of Jesus Christ to *be* the church He died to establish.

Our decaying culture needs committed disciples of Christ— followers, not just fans.

MAKING DISCIPLES

One recent article published by the Institute for the Study of American Evangelicals of Wheaton College suggests there are nearly 100 million evangelical Christians in America, comprising about 35 percent of our entire nation.[1] Now if that's true, it poses a great problem: If there are so many Christians, why do we still have all of this mess? The answer is simple—we are running short on disciples.

After He rose from the dead, the Lord Jesus Christ took steps to ensure that there would be disciples. He immediately called a meeting held on a hillside in Galilee. According to Matthew 28:16, Jesus' eleven remaining disciples showed up. Secondly, according to 1 Corinthians 15:6, more than five hundred additional people showed up at another appearance. But there was a third group of people included in that large post-Resurrection meeting—and that group includes you and me. At the end of his meeting with the Eleven, Jesus said, "I am with you always, even to the end of the age" (Matthew 28:20). Since the age Jesus was speaking of hasn't ended yet, and since you and I are living in that age, we are also part of that historic occasion.

Before we go any further, let's read the "minutes" of Jesus' meeting:

The eleven disciples proceeded to Galilee, to the mountain which Jesus had designated. When they saw Him, they worshiped Him; but some were doubtful. And Jesus came up and spoke to them, saying, "All authority has been given to Me in heaven and on earth. Go therefore and make disciples of all the nations, baptizing them in the name of the Father and the Son and the Holy Spirit, teaching them to observe all that I commanded you; and lo, I am with you always, even to the end of the age." (Matthew 28:16–20)

I doubt you have ever read any church committee minutes like those. But despite the fact that this meeting includes all the saints in church history from Pentecost to today, we still don't have enough committed disciples.

Now if there is a discipleship problem in the church, we can be sure it has nothing to do with the church's Head and the Leader of this meeting, Jesus Christ. In fact, Jesus said that "all authority" had been given to Him in heaven and on earth. He is in charge. In fact, that's what the word "authority" in Matthew 28:18 actually means. It means being in charge—power in the right hands. When Jesus said that all authority was His in heaven and on earth, He was saying that He is the right Person to wield that power.

The words "heaven and earth" remind us of the prayer Jesus taught His disciples to pray: "Your will be done, on earth as it is in heaven" (Matthew 6:10). According to Jesus, a disciple's first concern should be that God's will is done on earth just as it is done in heaven. So how is

God's will done in heaven? Completely and perfectly, no questions, no objections, no debate. In fact, Satan was the only one to ever challenge God's will in heaven, and he was kicked out.

So Jesus' plan is that there would be a group of people on earth who make up his global church and who reflect the nature of heaven. That way, no matter where people live, if they want to know what is going on in heaven, all they have to do is check out their local church. God's people are to be earthly models of heaven's reality.

WHAT ABOUT US?

Since Jesus has already achieved victory and Satan is a defeated enemy, what is our role as followers of His who have been left behind here on earth? Jesus answered that with a very succinct answer on one occasion when He and the disciples were nearing Jerusalem just before His crucifixion.

The disciples thought that Jesus was going to Jerusalem to take over and set up His kingdom right then. Jesus knew what they were thinking, so He told them the parable of the nobleman who went on a long journey and left certain sums of money with his servants. Then the nobleman said something very interesting. He told them, "Occupy till I come" (Luke 19:13 KJV). In other words, "Do business for me while I'm gone. I'll be back."

I like that word "occupy." As Jesus' disciples, we're like the occupying army that a conquering general leaves behind in the conquered country to maintain stability and progression after the battle has been won. Even though Satan is a defeated enemy, he still has a lot of fight left in him, and he wants to take as many people down with him as he can. So our task as Jesus' occupying force is more involved than just sitting back and keeping an eye on things. The purpose of the church is to make disciples, not just add names to the roll or increase small group Bible study attendance.

BIG NUMBERS, SMALL IMPACT

It is possible today that some megachurches in our country couldn't find fifty true disciples—and that in some small churches many members are disciples. The cost of the building says nothing about how well it produces true disciples. Our megachurch phenomena in our culture over the last two decades has produced a lot of good in many ways, but it has also produced a lot of ineffective religion as well. It provides an easier way for members of the body of Christ to check off a list rather than commit a life.

The difference between the church of the first century and the church today is that when the early disciples showed up, they made an impact and they often faced difficulties as a result.

Right after Paul was saved, he had to leave Damascus hidden in a basket that friends lowered over the city wall late at night to keep his enemies from killing him (Acts 9:23–25). In Thessalonica, the enemies of Christ mistreated the man in whose house Paul was staying (Acts 17:5–9). Paul was always starting something, but not because he was a troublemaker. Wherever Paul went, things started to happen because he preached Jesus. He lived and breathed Jesus and expected others to do the same—and Jesus is often polarizing. Yet far too often today, when people from church show up, they only do so to relax and serve a cappuccino. There's nothing polarizing about a cup of coffee.

The world is ignoring the church these days in a myriad of ways and on a myriad of issues. What's worse is that some members of the church aren't interested in Jesus either; they've grown disinterested in Him. You can't be like Jesus on your job, in your neighborhood— and, possibly, even within your church—and not have some opposition, whether that be in the physical realm from the people around you or in the spiritual realm from Satan and his demons. If you're having an easy time of it, if Satan never bothers you, you'd better check the direction you're walking and the faith you're talking. You may not be walking with and talking about Jesus Christ as Lord.

In biblical days in Rome, Christians would be brought before the magistrates because they were declaring Jesus as Lord in both speech and actions. The term "Lord" means supreme ruler or authority. The Roman authorities would attempt to

If you're having an easy time of it, if Satan never bothers you, you'd better check the faith you're talking.

get the Christians to declare Caesar as Lord, and deny Jesus as supreme ruler and authority.

Believing in Jesus didn't get the Christians hung or tossed to the lions for sport. Believing in Jesus as the rightful ruler and Lord did. There's a difference.

Frequently throughout the New Testament the disciples and the apostles regularly referred to themselves as slaves. The book of Romans opens up with these words: "Paul, a bond-servant of Christ Jesus" (Romans 1:1). A bond servant is translated from the Greek *doulos*, which literally means "slave." A slave is someone who has a master, or a Lord. Declaring Jesus as your Savior takes you to heaven, but declaring Jesus as your Master, or Lord, brings heaven to you. It is in acknowledging your rightful place under Jesus as His *doulos*, or slave, that you get His delivering power on earth.

The reason why we may not be seeing more of God's rescue and deliverance in individual lives, homes, churches, and in our country is because we have Jesus positioned as a good man, but not as our Lord. We, the collective body of Christ, are not His slaves—we are not his disciples. Keep in mind that the job of a slave is to do whatever the Master says to do. It's as straightforward as that.

Unfortunately, today Jesus must compete with many other masters. But Jesus is not willing to be one among many. He is not willing to be part of an association or club. Neither is He willing to be relegated as a personal assistant. Jesus as Lord means that Jesus is to be the supreme ruler and master. He calls the shots, and He is to be acknowledged in everything that is done.

Jesus as Lord means that He is to be the supreme ruler and master. He calls the shots.

The sermons I preach at our church in Dallas are recorded on master compact disks. These masters are then put on a duplicating machine to produce CDs for our church members and to go out all over the world through our national ministry, The Urban Alternative.

There is only one master CD for each message, but of course this master can produce any number of duplicates. It's interesting that the duplicating machine into which the blank CDs are placed to receive the master's message is called the "slave unit." The task of the slave unit is not to create its own message, or to distort the message it is receiving, but to faithfully record and play back what is said on the master. That's a picture of the discipleship process. Jesus is the Master, and we are His slaves (Ephesians 6:6).

THE LEARNERS WHO INFLUENCE THE WORLD

Discipleship was not a new idea in the New Testament times. It was a well-established concept in the Greek world in the centuries before Christ. The word disciple means "learner, student," and the Greeks had disciples in the realm of philosophy.

Plato, often called the "father of philosophy," developed a system of thought that dealt with issues of epistemology, or how we gain knowledge, and issues related to the meaning of life. Plato discipled his student Aristotle, who took what he had learned and built "gymnasiums," or academies.

In the ancient world, gymnasiums were not only arenas for sporting events. They were also training centers to teach students Plato's thought and the system developed by Aristotle, known as Aristotelian logic. The students thus trained were "gymnatized," which is the verb form of the Greek word for gymnasium.

So successful was this discipling process that it allowed the Greeks to influence the whole Greco-Roman world. This process was called "Hellenization," in which people who were not Greek began to adopt Greek thinking, language, and culture. That was all part of this concept of discipleship.

The New Testament picked up this concept and put it in a spiritual context so we would know what it means to be a disciple of Jesus Christ. Discipleship involves an apprenticeship in which the apprentice, or student, is brought toward a particular goal. Each disciple is to influence his world, echoing the lessons of his master.

In Matthew 10:24–25, Jesus described what a disciple should look like. We read, "A disciple is not above his teacher, nor a slave above his master. It is enough for the disciple that he become like his teacher, and the slave like his master."

THE GOAL

The goal of discipleship is conformity to the Savior, being transformed into the image or likeness of Christ (Romans 8:29), and then likewise sharing His person with others.

A pastor friend of mine was visiting a college campus a number of years ago and saw my son Anthony walking off in the distance. Not knowing Anthony was a student there, he later told me that he knew that had to be my son simply because of the resemblance. He was right, of course—it was Anthony Jr.

Friends, people ought to be able to see you from a distance and say, "That person has to be a follower of Jesus Christ." They ought to be able to tell you belong to Christ by what you say, how you act, and who you are. The family resemblance ought to be obvious. That is discipleship. It means to so pattern your life after Christ, to follow Him so closely, that you reflect Him well.

If enough of us will commit to follow Christ as His disciples, then we will gain the ability to influence our culture and our country, turning our nation to God. Otherwise, we are guilty of helping to destroy America simply by our spiritual neglect, inertia, and a lack of commitment.

Jesus makes it plain in the Great Commission that discipleship begins with a commitment to evangelism. This is the responsibility of "going" and sharing the good news of the death and resurrection of Jesus Christ with the unsaved with the goal of bringing the hearer to faith in Him for their salvation. If we can talk to men about our preferred political candidate or sports team, then we certainly should have no problem talking to people about our Savior.

The second aspect of discipleship is baptism. This is more than getting people wet. It refers to reclassifying believers so that they publically identify themselves as followers of Christ. Baptism means you are no longer a secret agent Christian or spiritual CIA representative. It means you are a visible verbal follower of Christ reflecting His attitudes and actions, character, and conduct in every aspect of life.

The third aspect of discipleship is teaching. However, Jesus makes it clear that this teaching is not merely imparting theological concepts, but rather showing how biblical truths are to be utilized and applied in everyday life. Thus Jesus' commands are to be observed, not merely understood.

Jesus then makes it clear that when this understanding of discipleship is taking place in the culture, then His special and unique presence will be with us resulting in greater influence and impact in society. Therefore, the presence or absence of disciples is directly related to the level of Jesus' active, powerful presence in our society.

THE ROLE OF PRAYER

On the day the Titanic was scheduled to sail, the second officer was removed from the crew. In his pocket was the key to the locker that housed the binoculars that were used for the sailor in the crow's nest to see far ahead of the ship. Because the key was missing, the sailor was limited to what his human eyes could see. Because he could not see the iceberg, 1,522 people lost their lives in the chilly waters of the Atlantic on April 14, 1912, when the Titanic sank.

Just as tragic as the missing key was that the lifeboats designed to save people from dying were only half full. Even though the people in the boats could hear those who were freezing to death in the waters some distance from them, most of the boats did not go near them in an effort to save anyone else. Instead, they deafened their ears as they sat secure in their own salvation only, unwilling to risk returning to the dangerous scene.

The body of Christ must do better than those in the lifeboats on the fateful day as the Titanic sank. We must be stirred in the area of evangelism in order to take the risk and reach out to those who are lost. One thing that can light the passion of evangelism in our hearts at a greater and more aggressive level is the act of prayer.

If you ask me, "Tony, how can I get a burden to reach out to the lost and overcome my fears of evangelizing?", my answer would be to start praying. Pray for unsaved family members, friends, and coworkers by name. Ask God to break your heart over their condition and give you "divine appointments" to share Christ with them and the boldness to speak for Him. Pray also for boldness and courage in your own heart. Pray that the Lord will give you spiritual eyes to view humanity and the lost the way He does. Let your gratitude for your salvation be a fire that lights your desire to share that salvation with others.

And, by the way, if you feel fearful at times, you are not alone. Even Paul, the great evangelist, asked the Ephesians to pray that he would have the boldness necessary to proclaim the gospel.

Paul's prayer request is worth quoting here because it would make a great prayer for you to pray: "Pray ... that utterance may be given to me in the opening of my mouth, to make known with boldness the mystery of the gospel ... that in proclaiming it I may speak boldly, as I ought to speak" (Ephesians 6:19–20).

The Bible says that Christians are no longer to live for themselves (see 2 Corinthians 5:15). Many of us are not seeing the power of God at work because we're living for ourselves when God wants us to have a heart for others that's as big as the needy world we live in. When we start praying for people's salvation and discipleship, we won't have a hard time reaching out to the spiritually lost and making room for them in the lifeboat, because we will realize that the church's witness is a life-and-death issue.

If you and I and a few million other Christians will become burdened to actively evangelize not only in our churches but in our daily lives, we'll have a big part of the answer to the question of whether believers in Christ are actually followers and not just fans. And whether we are collectively contributing to the destruction or restoration of America.

12

A Call for National Revival

Every two years nations around the globe send their strongest, most elite athletes to compete against others at what is known as the Olympics—either the summer or winter games. Individual athletes at the top of their game in their particular event go head-to-head with the world's best. On display for the world to see are their individual prowess, their individual determination, their individual commitment, and their individual abilities.

Yet when the gold medalist stands on the platform, he or she is not asked, "What is your favorite song?" The winning athlete does not get to choose which song will be played as the three flags of the first, second, and third finishers are raised. Instead, the national anthem for the nation of the gold medal winner plays loudly.

The champion of the event was the one who sacrificed, practiced, and competed, yet he or she accepts it is the country that is honored because the athlete represents something much larger than himself. The athlete is just one of many who make up a nation to whom the competitor has pledged his loyalty.

Growing up in America, we were regularly reminded to whom we belonged each time we said the pledge of allegiance or participated in the singing of our national anthem in school or before sporting or civic events. It was clear that our country did not want us to forget that we are Americans. We recited the pledge each day, allowing it to sink in, enabling each one of us to fully understand that no matter who we were, or what our background was, our history, gender, culture, or color, we belonged to this land called the United States of America.

Even though the pledge had nothing directly to do with what was going on at that particular event or in the classroom, America wanted us to know that it was only going on, and we were only able to participate in it, because we belonged to its kingdom.

THE KINGDOM AGENDA

The foundational philosophy behind all I do, write, teach, or preach is the kingdom agenda. The kingdom agenda is *the visible manifestation of the comprehensive rule of God over every area of life*. It is a reminder that we, as followers of Jesus Christ, belong to another realm—an eternal kingdom—and allegiance is in another order, and no matter where we live, work, or travel, we are citizens of God's kingdom.

The unifying theme of Scripture is the glory of God through the advancement of His kingdom in history. God's kingdom has been designed that we might become kingdom disciples and that we might make kingdom disciples, thus mirroring God's image and rule on earth. That is still God's goal, even though sin has distorted His original design.

This kingdom goal, however, can only be reached as people operate under His authority. And it is to be reached in each of His four covenantal spheres of engagement: individual, family, church, and society.

A covenant is a spiritually binding relationship established by God. Each of these four covenants has its own requirements and promises. As each one operates underneath God's authority, then God's transforming presence and power is made manifest through them. Conversely, as His divinely designed covenants operate independently of His authority, chaos replaces order. What we are experiencing today is the refusal of mankind to comprehensively recognize and reflect His will on earth "as it is in heaven."

The kingdom agenda is God's blueprint for how life ought to be lived. It needs to remain at the forefront of our thinking in order to fully penetrate our choices and decisions, thus bringing about the full realization of its covenantal blessings and authority.

I believe that one of the reasons we don't take our outreach and influence responsibilities more seriously in our nation is because we don't fully understand the message of the kingdom. As a result, this has caused much, if not most, of the confusion in our churches in our land. Not because people don't speak of the kingdom, but because far too much of their speech is in esoteric, theological "code words" that seem unrelated to the realities of life in the here and now.

The absence of a comprehensive understanding of the kingdom has led to a deterioration in our world of cosmic proportions. People live segmented, compartmentalized lives because they lack a kingdom worldview. Families disintegrate because they exist for their own fulfillment rather than for the kingdom. Churches are having a limited impact on society because they fail to understand that the goal of the church is not the church itself but the kingdom. This myopic perspective keeps the church divided, ingrown, and unable to transform the cultural landscape in any significant way.

And because this is so, society at large has nowhere to turn to find solid solutions to the perplexing challenges that confront us today—troubling problems such as crime, racism, poverty, and a myriad of other ills which continue to show up in our politics and policies in voting booths year after year. Yet for each and every issue, God's kingdom agenda provides an alternative—another way to see and live life in this world. It transcends the politics of men and offers the solutions of heaven.

THE KINGDOM'S RULER AND REALM

Throughout the Bible, the kingdom of God is His rule, His plan, and His program. God's kingdom is all-embracing. It covers everything. The Greek word the Bible uses for kingdom is *basileia*, which basically means a "rule" or "authority." Included in this definition is the idea of power. So when we talk about a kingdom, we're talking first about a king and a ruler.

Now if there's a ruler, there also have to be "rulees," or kingdom subjects. A kingdom also includes a realm; that is, a sphere over which the king rules. Finally, if you're going to have a ruler, rulees, and a realm, you also need kingdom regulations, guidelines that govern the relationship between the ruler and the subjects. These are necessary so the rulees will know whether they are doing what the ruler wants done.

God's kingdom includes all of these elements. He is the absolute Ruler of His domain, which encompasses all of creation. And His authority is total. A kingdom perspective does not view man's condition first and then assign to God what we feel would best reflect Him. Rather, a kingdom perspective ascertains what God has said and then aligns itself with that despite our inability to always understand God's processes.

At the heart of the kingdom agenda philosophy is the fact that there should never be a separation between the sacred and the secular. All of life is spiritual since all of life is to come under God's rule. Therefore, every issue—whether social, political, economic, educational, environmental, or others is to mirror God's principles related to the specific area and thus reflect and promote His agenda in history.

God has made Jesus Christ the sovereign over all of mankind's kingdoms (Matthew 28:18; Colossians 1:13–18). His rule is to be represented in history by those who are a part of His kingdom and who have been delegated the responsibility of dispensing His rule to the nations (Matthew 28:19; Ephesians 1:21–23). Christian living and influence should reflect this reality.

Colossians 1:13 says that everybody who has trusted the Lord Jesus Christ as Savior has been transferred from the domain of darkness to the kingdom of light in "His beloved Son." If you are a believer in Jesus Christ, your allegiance has been changed. You are no longer to follow the world's ways, but Christ.

THE PROBLEM AND THE SOLUTION

The problem in our society today is that too many people are looking for "salvation by government." They are looking to force God's hand, way, and will into the box of elected officials. They want a kingdom they can schedule, program, and understand, thus putting their hope in the political realm. But God warns us what happens when we put our confidence in kings (1 Samuel 8:9–18). There is no such thing as salvation by government (Judges 8:22–23).

Even so, the Democrats are looking for a Democratic savior, the Republicans are looking for a Republican savior, and the Independents are looking for an Independent savior. However, God alone sits as the potentate of the universe, saying—as He did through the prophet in Ezekiel 43—"I am the only Savior in town."

Therefore what we need in our nation today is a radical, comprehensive, covenantal return to the God of the Bible—our true and only Savior, and this can be initiated through a collective national solemn assembly in which we seek revival in each of the four covenantal spheres: individual, family, church, and society. In addition to a national solemn assembly, we need to integrate and influence our culture through all possible media. Almost everyone recognizes the fact that the task of national renewal in the areas of faith and freedom is too big for any one group or church to accomplish effectively. It will require the collective cooperation of the masses to leave a lasting impact for good.

One way of getting a jump-start on this collective impact is by identifying the Christian agencies and individuals who already have intellectual affinity and integration within the spheres of typical American society: education, healthcare, entertainment, the news media, publishing, government, and business. Add to that the agencies of research, family issues, law, national security, economics, community affairs, and social activism. The primary goal of such identification is to take advantage of opportunities of cross-pollinating efforts while also sharing research on cultural trends and indicators. In doing so, we provide a more synergistic approach to shaping the moral framework of our land.

Some of the goals of this partner-platform might include:

+ To awaken and initiate the desire for national revival, personal responsibility, spiritual integration, and progressive reformation.
+ To develop a national strategy of social impact, scalable and implementable across cultural, geographical, and class lines.
+ To increase the effectiveness of the mobilization and management of American Christian resources for national kingdom impact.
+ To develop a national ongoing prayer movement to support the initiatives.
+ To build and promote collaboration among churches, nonprofits, training institutions, and agencies.
+ To facilitate research and discussion on national trends within the various mediums in order to stimulate strategic influence.
+ To reduce wasteful duplication of efforts.

+ To create a forum for the sharing of strategies and techniques while providing responsible forecasting.
+ To produce artistically excellent, compelling means of storytelling to encourage kingdom thinking and personal responsibility through mainstream distribution channels.
+ To leverage social media and YouTube to transform thinking toward national renewal and kingdom values.
+ To devise a corporate approach to deal with collective felt needs.
+ To encourage thinking about community and national impact as also a local church strategy rather than solely a parachurch strategy.
+ To promote and gather a National Solemn Assembly, drawing together spiritual leaders and laity to seek God's face and invoke His hand in our land.

EXPERIENCING NATIONAL RENEWAL

Over the years and even in the past decade, we have had localized gatherings of believers seeking God's face in order to invoke His hand of involvement in our nation. People have met in cities, churches, and their homes to call on God and access heaven's intervention in our nation. Many, if not most, of these gatherings lasted one night, one Sunday, or perhaps two Sundays back-to-back. Yet in the busyness of the American lifestyle, it is easy for these experiences to be lumped into another long list of good things to do, and—as a result—lose the collective impact they were intended to have.

Likewise, because many, if not most, of these gatherings occurred segmented by denomination, church, or location, we did not experience renewal on the greater level that it is so desperately needed.

I have also noticed that while there has been much emphasis on 2 Chronicles 7:14 reminding believers that, "[If] My people who are called by My name [will] humble themselves and pray . . . I . . . will forgive their sin and will heal their land," there has been less ardent proclamation and awareness of the variety of elements that historically comprised collective solemn assemblies. As I mentioned in an earlier chapter, the "fast" God chooses goes deeper than a prayer said without a meal. It even goes deeper than confessing sins. Rather, it involves the intentional application of His two greatest commandments of loving Him and others.

Have we gathered as groups to seek God's face in our land? Yes. Have we met in churches every so often and scattered across our nation to seek revival? Yes. But have we ever done this collectively and comprehensively with unity from our nation's spiritual leaders? No. Have we ever done it coupled with the intentional applicational realities of carrying out God's command of love? Not that I'm aware of.

It is time for a comprehensive season of seeking our Lord's hand and face in our great land.

Lastly, have we truly experienced God's hand of national revival in the last century? I would also argue—no. If we are, as His people, going to seek His face—we will need to set aside personal agenda, organizations, denominations, structures, and the like, and come together once and for all as the body of disciples whom Christ died to procure, and call on the name of our great God and King.

Have you ever noticed how "special interest groups" in our country carry far more weight in influencing our land (policies, opinions, etc.) even though their numbers are but a small fraction of the number of evangelicals and believers in America? The reason they carry so much weight and influence is because they unite. We may have the numbers in our favor as an overall body of believers, but we have rarely, if ever, truly united over anything.

It is time to set our preferences and egos aside and go before the Lord as one body. It is also time for more than an evening event or

Sunday morning assembly. It is time for a comprehensive season of seeking our Lord's hand and face in our great land. One of the ways to do this is to focus an entire segment of time—whether that be a week or several days—on each of the four covenantal areas of God's involvement with humanity: individual, family, church, and society.

A PROLONGED SOLEMN ASSEMBLY

Every year in January for the last several decades, I have led our congregation in a weeklong solemn assembly starting on Sunday morning and culminating with a "Break the Fast" breakfast on Saturday morning. This solemn assembly involves giving up some personal physical need or desire every day to call on God for His presence throughout the year. It also involves meeting together as a church body six times in the week, and as individual families one night.

I'm not proposing this as a standard process for carrying out a national solemn assembly, but I am proposing that we enter into something that is more comprehensive and more collective nationwide than a gathering on a Sunday or two.

If every serious Bible believing church would do their own solemn assembly simultaneously with the others—whether that be for a solid week, or spread out over four weeks allowing time for personal reflection during the weekdays—we would seek God as a nation together. If church and organizational leadership would come together in humility and unity, we could actually see the hand of God move in our midst in a way we may have never imagined.

The problem is not merely our waiting on God to involve Himself in our country's demise, but it is also that God is waiting on us to call on Him collectively, and according to His prescribed manner. A couple of logistical suggestions exist for how we might carry this out nationally, which include:

Schedule option one: A four-day national solemn assembly to be carried out the third week in January in the following manner:

- *Sunday.* Churches across the nation teach the practice of the solemn assembly while individuals continue to pray for personal revival.
- *Monday.* Churches convene with families for family revival.
- *Tuesday.* Churches convene with their leadership teams for a time of solemn assembly while congregants are equipped with the tools to pray for God's hand in their leadership and church revival.
- *Wednesday.* Churches are united via a televised simulcast to participate in the culmination of the week through a national focus of prayer and seeking God for national revival.

Schedule option two: A four-week national solemn assembly to be carried out beginning the first Sunday in January in the following manner:

- *Week One.* A Sunday gathering focuses on matters of personal revival, followed up with study notes, questions, and prayer guide for personal time Monday through Saturday related to individual confession, renewal, vision, and praise.
- *Week Two.* A Sunday gathering focuses on matters of family revival, followed up with study notes, questions, and prayer guide for personal time Monday through Saturday related to familial confession, renewal, vision, and praise. (Note: For singles, "family" can refer to the future family or primary family.)
- *Week Three.* A Sunday gathering focuses on matters of church revival, followed up with study notes, questions, and prayer guide for personal time Monday through Saturday

related to church confession, renewal, vision, and praise.

- *Week Four.* A Sunday gathering focuses on matters of societal revival, followed up with study notes, questions, and prayer guide for personal time Monday through Saturday related to societal confession, renewal, vision, and praise, and culminating in a national collective solemn assembly held in one location, and/or groups of community gatherings of churches.

Of course these are logistical suggestions only, but any approach to unite to address the underlying spiritual issues in our land and let our collective voices be heard on high will be a wonderful way to begin to turn our nation to God. We are too far down the road in our country of turning away from God for us to just ignore it, or simply bemoan it, and do nothing about it from a biblically strategic vantage point. We must set aside our personal, church, denominational, and organizational biases and egos, and come together underneath the overarching rule and call of Jesus Christ. We must do this to seek God's favor in turning our nation to Him.

PRACTICING THE HEALING ART

The story is told of a man and his wife who were driving home from their honeymoon when an oncoming truck crashed into their vehicle. They had been driving in a rural area with very little traffic on the roads. So when the man saw his new wife bloody and bruised from the accident, he quickly picked her up in his arms and started walking toward the nearest farmhouse.

Once he had reached the long, winding driveway of a nearby home, he noticed on the mailbox the name, "Dr. Thomas Brown." Hopeful that this meant that Dr. Brown was indeed a medical practitioner, the man quickened his pace up the gravel driveway to the home.

Once at the house's threshold, the weary husband saw another sign hung squarely in the middle of his door. Again, it read, "Dr. Thomas Brown." *Surely this man must be a medical doctor,* he thought, *or he wouldn't have a sign placed so prominently on his door.*

The desperate husband knocked incessantly, having no patience to wait for someone to come. His wife still lay unconscious and bleeding in his arms, even as he sought to pound on the door. After a few moments, a man came to the door and opened it wide. Looking at the woman who was injured, bruised, and covered with blood, the resident shook his head and said, "I'm sorry."

"Do something for her!" the new husband yelled. "You're a doctor, right?"

"I used to be," the man standing at the door replied. "But I don't practice anymore."

The new husband stood bewildered, not quite knowing what to say. After all, he saw the placard on the mailbox and the door. Surely this man could help.

"I'm sorry," the man said again, and then shut the door.

The newlywed holding his dying wife in his arms pounded on the door once more. When the elderly man opened it again, the new husband had only these words to say: "If you no longer practice, then take down your sign!"

Friends and fellow believers, Jesus Christ came to empower His body with wisdom, love, and the restorative strength that will impact and influence a lost and dying world. We have signs and steeples put up all over our land—more so than ever before—yet we are having less of a healing influence on our nation than ever before.

It's time for us to start practicing the healing art of prayer, fasting, discipleship, and disciple making once again, which can begin by a collective call for God's favor, forgiveness, and grace through a national solemn assembly. Either we need to start fully practicing and delivering what we have been put here to do in the midst of our decaying land, or we need to take down our signs.

CONCLUSION

A Declaration of Dependence

Since national revival begins with Christians comprehensively functioning under God's rule, it is past time for a new declaration. America was born out of a desire for independence from the tyranny of England. But spiritual revival demands just the opposite. It requires verbal and visible dependence on God. If we want God to bless America, then America must first bless God. This means His people must first totally dedicate allegiance to Him through the four covenantal kingdom spheres He has established. Those four spheres are personal, familial, the church, and national.

1. A PERSONAL DECLARATION OF DEPENDENCE

Every Christian must decide to no longer serve two masters. God makes it clear that we cannot have the world and have Him at the same time (1 John 2:15–17). Practically this means that God's person, principles, and precepts must be brought to bear on all of our decisions (not just the so-called religious ones). He must be Lord of all of life. Each day must begin with a commitment to Him above all else, and He is to be consulted in prayer on all matters of life (Luke 9:23).

2. A FAMILY DECLARATION OF DEPENDENCE

Heads of households must make the declaration of Joshua the slogan for their own home: "As for me and my house, we will serve the Lord" (Joshua 24:15). The dinner table must again become the central place for reviewing and applying kingdom principles (Psalm 128:3). Couples must reconnect themselves to their biblical roles and hate divorce as much as God does (Malachi 2:14). There must be a regular review of the progress the family is making at adhering to godly principles, and the family altar must become central in the home.

3. THE CHURCHES' DECLARATION OF DEPENDENCE

Local churches must recommit themselves to their primary responsibility of making disciples and not be satisfied with simply expanding their membership. Jesus doesn't need more fans. He wants more followers. Programs must be evaluated in terms of whether they are growing visible, verbal followers of Christ and not by how many people are entertained by church events. This means that there must be loving accountability incorporated into the life of the church. In addition there must be a radical return by church leadership to the authority of Scripture and priority of prayer as the foundation of church life (1 Timothy 2:8–9). The church must have regular, unified sacred gatherings to keep the focus on our absolute dependency on God.

4. A NATIONAL DECLARATION OF DEPENDENCE

The church must again become the conscience of the government. Through its national solemn assembly it should clearly and respectfully call political leaders to God's principles for government (Romans 13:1–7), which means we cannot be so entrenched with political parties that we are not free to speak truth to power. It also means we must begin speaking with one voice, so the nation sees a unified church and not one divided by faith. In addition, we should so overwhelm the culture with good works that the benefit we bring cannot be overlooked or denied (Matthew 5:16). Finally, all attempts to remove God from the marketplace ought to be resisted while we simultaneously bring our public officials in prayer before the throne of grace (1 Timothy 2:1–3).

As God's kingdom agenda is manifested simultaneously through His four covenantal spheres, in a spirit of dependence on Him, then we will have done our part in welcoming the glory of our great God to be among us and for God to bring the revival we and our nation so very desperately need, before it's too late.

We invite you to join with others to go online and sign a National Declaration of Dependence at www.turninganationtoGod.com. While there, you can also download your own personal, family, and church declaration of dependence to sign, frame, and display.

NOTES

Chapter 1: When the King Is Your Problem

1. Oliver W. Price, "The Welch Revival of 1904–1905," cited at the library of the website openheaven.com; see http://www.openheaven.com/library/history/wales.htm.

2. Examples abound in the Old Testament. See 2 Chronicles 12:1-8, Rehoboam; 2 Chronicles 15:1-19, Asa; 2 Chronicles 20:1-29, Jehoshaphat; 2 Chronicles 29–31, Hezekiah; 2 Chronicles 34, Josiah; Ezra 10:7–10a, Ezra; Nehemiah 8–9, Nehemiah; Joel 1–2, Joel.

3. "Billion-Dollar Weather/Climate Disasters: Overview," The National Climatic Data Center of the National Oceanic and Atmospheric Administration, at www.ncdc.noaa.gov/billions/. Figures for all years have been adjusted to reflect the consumer price index of specific years.

Chapter 2: Returning with All Your Heart

1. Judges 10:10–19; 1 Samuel 7:5–6; 1 Samuel 10:17–27; ; 2 Kings 23:3; 1 Chronicles 13–18; 2 Chronicles 5–7; 2 Chronicles 15:9–15; 2 Chronicles 20:3–13; 2 Chronicles 23:16; 2 Chronicles 29:3–36; 2 Chronicles 34:31–33; Ezra 6:6–12; Ezra 8:21–23; Nehemiah 8; Esther 4:5–17; Joel 1:13; 2:12–17.

2. Genesis 35:1–15; Exodus 19:10–19; Joshua 7; 2 Chronicles 30; Jonah 3.

3. Leviticus 23:15–21; Numbers 28:26–31; Acts 2:1, also known as sacred assemblies, holy assemblies, and holy convocations.

4. 2 Chronicles 12:1–8; 2 Chronicles 15:1–19; 2 Chronicles 20:1–29; 2 Chronicles 29–31; 2 Chronicles 34; Ezra 10:7–9; Nehemiah 8–9; Joel 1–2.

Chapter 3: The Unshakeable Kingdom

1. http://www.christianitytoday.com/ct/2013/september-web-only/secrets-of-giving-church.html, accessed June 14, 2014, "The Secrets of a Giving Church," Christianity Today, Abby Stocker, September 6, 2013.

Chapter 8: Igniting the Fire of Revival

1. "Report: Government Subsidizing Junk Food Ingredients," The Lead with Jake Tapper, July 27, 2013, CNN-TV; at http://thelead.blogs.cnn.com/2013/07/17/report-government-subsidizing-junk-food-ingredients/.

2. The World Health Organization lists poor diet as one factor common to those unemployed due to "a health condition . . . and personal and environmental factors (e.g., negative attitudes, inaccessible transportation and public buildings)." "Disability and Health," Fact Sheet 352; at http://www.who.int/mediacentre/factsheets/fs352/en/.

Chapter 9: The Danger of Independence

1. "Milestones: 1776–1783; The Declaration of Independence," U.S. Department of State, Office of the Historian, at https://history.state.gov/milestones/1776-1783/declaration.

Chapter 10: The Partnership of Church and State

1. See the book of Esther.

2. Andrew Small, "Faith-Based Initiatives: An Appropriate Alliance between Governments and Religion?" January 18, 2010; at http://truboverbal.blogspot/2010/01/faith-based-initiatives-appropriate.html.

Chapter 11: Creating Followers, Not Just Fans

1. Larry Ekridge, "How Many Evangelicals Are There?" Institute for the Study of American Evangelicals, Wheaton College, http://www.wheaton.edu/ISAE/Defining-Evangelicalism/How-Many-Are-There. See also Frank Newport and Joseph Carroll, "Another Look at Evangelicals in America Today," Gallup, December 2, 2005, at www.gallup.com/poll/20242/Another-Look-Evangelicals-America-Today.aspx.

Appendix A: A Strategy for National Impact

1. Bob Smietana, "Statistical Illusion: New study confirms that we go to church much less than we say," April 1, 2006, http://www.christianitytoday.com/ct/2006/april/32.85.html.

2. George Barna, *Transforming Children into Spiritual Champions* (Ventura, Calif.: Regal, 2003), 12.

3. Ibid., 14.

4. Bill Whitaker, CBSNews.com, "High School Dropouts Costly for American Economy," May 26, 2010, http://www.cbsnews.com/ stories/2010/05/28/eveningnews/ main6528227.shtml#ixzz1PN htcbfg.

5. "Counting It Up: The Public Costs of Teen Childbearing," The National Campaign to Prevent Teen and Unwanted Pregnancies at http://www.the-nationalcampaign.org/why-it-matters/public-cost.

6. C. Rouse, "Labor Market Consequences of an Inadequate Education," paper prepared for the symposium on the Social Costs of Inadequate Education, New York, October 24, 2005.

7. Jennifer Warren, Pew Center on the States, "One in 100: Behind Bars in America 2008," February 2008, 5, http://www.pewcenteronthestates.org/uploadedFiles/8015PCTS_Prison08_FINAL_2-1-1_FORWEB.pdf.

8. Pew Center on the States, "One in 31: The Long Reach of American Corrections" (Washington, DC: The Pew Charitable Trusts, March 2009) 11, http://www.pewcenteronthestates.org/uploadedFiles/PSPP_1in31_report_FINAL_WEB_3-26-09.pdf.

APPENDIX A

A Strategy for National Impact

Within the United States, the structure is already in place to address social problems in our communities. We don't need to create new institutions in order to implement viable and lasting solutions; we just need to leverage what we already have.

The church, in particular, exists as the best vehicle through which we find the necessary elements to achieve the purpose of social restoration, for a number of reasons.

First and most obvious, churches are located everywhere. In fact, there is an average of three churches for every public school in America.[1] Consequently, churches are closer to the needs of the people since they are located in the heart of the community. In addition, churches offer the largest volunteer force in our nation. Next, churches already have buildings for housing community programs. And finally, churches offer a spiritual and moral frame of reference for helping people make the right choices.

Since many of our communities' issues are ethical and moral at their foundation, churches represent the most natural social service agency to address these issues. The church provides holistic, long-term solutions that change how people think, which ultimately determines how they live.

One avenue of broadening the churches' impact on their communities is to recognize that churches and schools represent the social, educational, familial, and potentially spiritual nucleus of the community. As people and businesses come and go, churches and schools remain and are ready to accommodate newcomers to their neighborhoods. If these two institutions share common ground as well as longevity, a strategic alliance between the two can precipitate, to a greater degree, positive outcomes for children, youth, and families living in the community.

The spiritual must never be neglected if life is to function as our Creator intended. On the contrary, the spiritual must integrate with the social at every level. Yet doing this in a nation that has essentially removed God from our public schools and many arenas within our communities must be done in such a way that respects the institutional separation of church and state while also reflecting God's kingdom values through acts of service.

In essence, social services to those in need satisfies the law of love while building a relational bridge back to God and the ministries offered through the local body of Christ.

REACHING OUR YOUTH

Research verifies what we have frequently heard: those most open to conversion and life transformation are under the age of eighteen. Yet our operative values in the church, which are often revealed by our budgets, rarely take this knowledge seriously. It may be time to rethink our strategies.

George Barna, popular Christian pollster, points to survey results showing that the target of the modern-day church is adults. He says, "Adults are where the Kingdom action is."[2] However, as a result of extensive polling on the formation of worldview, habits, spiritual development, and the creation of patterns for making life choices, Barna concludes that outreach "to children is the single most strategic ministry in God's kingdom [and will have] . . . the greatest possible impact."[3]

Hundreds of millions of dollars are spent annually on programs, worldwide missions, and ministries aimed at adults when the ripest harvest is right across the street in the lives of young people longing to hear that they are valuable, skilled, and have both a future and a hope. The church is the corporate structure already set in place to deliver that message to a generation in need.

As we reach kids, they become the conduit to reaching the whole family and community. As the lives of children are impacted through churches' adoption of schools, the opportunity to access and influence families increases. To the degree that families are strengthened and stabilized, communities are positively affected. This is so because the breakdown of the family is the single greatest cause of social disintegration.

THE IMPACT OF SOCIAL ILLS

And social disintegration affects everyone in our nation, not just those living in our urban centers.

In 2010, taxpayers spent more than $8 billion annually on high school dropouts for public assistance programs such as food stamps.[4] More rent data show that teen pregnancies contribute to a $9.4 billion annual bill by way of public assistance, lost revenue, and increased health care costs.[5] High school dropouts earn an average of $260,000 less over the course of their lives than graduates—which equates to a cumulative loss of over $300 billion annually in earned taxable revenue.[6] Our prison population has nearly tripled the number of inmates since 1987 to the highest per capita rate in the world,[7] and now costs us over $52 billion a year on budgets for prisons.[8]

The consequences of society's problems reach us all and have contributed to our nation's standing on the brink of economic collapse.

Our society's problem is not solely our government's problem. It is the church's problem. It is our problem. Our mission field is not merely across the sea. It is across the street—in our own Jerusalem and Judea—in Detroit, Dallas, Baltimore, Miami, and in your community. To look away now may cost us more than we can afford. It may even cost us the futures of our own sons and daughters.

ONE CHURCH'S IMPACT IN THE COMMUNITY

Making an impact in our communities is not something that will come easily, though. As Martin Luther King Jr. once said, "Human progress is neither automatic nor inevitable . . . Every step toward the goal of justice requires sacrifice, suffering, and struggle; the tireless exertions and passionate concern of dedicated individuals."

One of the ways this is done is through community outreach by local churches. At our church (Oak Cliff Bible Fellowship) in Dallas, we have established one local model of church-school partnerships. Church-school partnerships consist of churches partnering with schools to seek to rebuild communities by comprehensively influencing the lives of urban youth and their families in addressing the education, health, economic, and social needs of hurting people based on spiritual principles.

This strategy began organically when I was a young pastor in what was then, and still is now, a predominantly urban community nearly three decades ago. A nearby high school was experiencing increased difficulties at the time, including delinquencies and low academic achievement. Gang activity had broken out, affecting all areas of performance within the school. The school principal decided to reach out to me for help. After receiving his phone call, I decided to visit the school with about twenty-five men from our church. The principal stopped all the classes and brought all the male students into the gymnasium, and we shared what it was like to be a real man.

After our time together, and after some of the men from the church began hanging out in the hallways—offering help and hope to those in need, plus accountability for those who wanted to cause trouble—the gang activity shut down. Student grades went up, delinquency was lowered, and the school acknowledged that the church connection was good for producing a more productive learning environment.

The principal later became the superintendent of the district of eighteen schools, and he requested our church's involvement in all eighteen schools. We then organized ourselves and adopted all of the schools, expanding our support services to each through mentoring, tutoring, and counseling, offering skills, training, and wraparound family support services. When the word got out to neighboring school districts, the eighteen schools soon became thirty-six, and eventually increased upwards of over sixty schools at this writing.

In addition, I initiated a meeting open to all the principals for Bible study, prayer, and spiritual encouragement. Held once a month at our church, we saw an average of thirty to forty in attendance over the years, and these biannual meetings continue to this day.

Many of the problems students had in school were an extension of brokenness in the homes. When we adopted the school, we also connected with the families, which in turn allowed us to connect at a deeper level with the entire community.

As our church positioned itself to be the major social service delivery system to the schools, the church provided an avenue to community transformation outside of the schools. This came through a pregnancy center, thrift store, educational center, food pantry, and much more. In fact, we have one of the largest functioning African-American pregnancy centers in the nation, providing not only prenatal care but also classes for both fathers and mothers.

We help people get an education and acquire job skills through our Technology Institute, then help them find jobs and get homes. We have a thrift store to help sustain and expand the economic growth in the community, as well as a Credit Union. We develop businesses and provide medical assistance on a regular basis free of charge to the community.

KINGDOM IMPACT IN THE CULTURE

Why do we do this? Because the church has been uniquely called to impact our culture for good. Churches around the country are to set the agenda for effecting positive values and beliefs. One way this can be done is by partnering with public schools and reaching into the community to promote a high quality of life in that area. When churches can set the agenda for the community, positive returns are compounded.

The mission of revitalizing and transforming communities begins with the individual along with a foundational truth—what a man thinks, he becomes. To put it another way, one's behavior is controlled by one's thoughts. If one's thought life is changed, the person is changed. Changed individuals transform families, and transformed families restore communities.

One of the most exciting aspects of this community outreach strategy is that it is scalable. The program works whether you have a church of forty members or forty thousand. Our church serves more than sixty public schools because we have enough members to sustain that level of impact. However, smaller churches can still make a significant impact in their communities by adopting just one public school (elementary, middle, or high school).

Additionally, the program is cost-effective because the basics of what you need are already in place at both the church and the public school. The actual program cost is contingent on the scope of services your church wants to offer and your capacity to deliver those services.

Whenever I go into a community to speak, I seek to rally the pastors and community leaders around a shared vision for a unified community-wide impact through the adoption of schools. My vision is to have ministerial associations, church denominations, or a group of churches in a local area band together to adopt all of the public schools in their community.

If every community adopted such a strategy, then over time the whole nation would be impacted through this bottom-up approach to community transformation.

OUTREACH STRATEGIES INTO YOUR COMMUNITY

At first sight, this may not appear to be addressing the depth of our racial divide in our nation today. However, a closer look at offering local social services rooted in a shared spiritual source reveals our greatest opportunity for applying the principle of unity. Teaching, preaching, singing, praying, writing, reading, and celebrating unity are all important elements of racial reconciliation. But actually rolling up our sleeves to work alongside each other toward a shared purpose and vision will not only bond us together but will also simultaneously undo elements of the generational effects of systemic racism.

A kingdom approach to social outreach encourages partnerships between churches of varying racial makeups in order to merge strength with strength to create a more viable impact in the community. Options for an outreach strategy in your community include *a public schools outreach, a technology and education institute, economic growth assistance, human needs assistance, youth programs, and a family-care pregnancy center.*

Public Schools Outreach. Promotes healthy school and home environments by building relationships with students through a combination of activities such as:

- *Mentoring.* A mentoring program seeks to implement character development while creating a sense of belonging among family, community, and peers. Mentoring also provides a means of surrogate parenting, to some degree, as needed. Mentors are either assigned as a group mentor (one adult mentor with a group of up to four same-sex young people) or as a team mentor (several adults working with small groups of young people). Mentors meet weekly on campus during school hours to discuss current needs and/or issues along with strategies toward making healthy choices.

+ *Tutoring.* Tutoring involves one-on-one assistance in the area of reading, language arts, and/or math.

+ *Life skills education.* This addresses a wide range of topics including sexual abstinence, anger and violence control, continuing in school, and substance abuse prevention.

+ *Annual back-to-school rallies.* Such rallies bring students together at the church for entertainment, promoting a drug-free and stay-in-school message, while also introducing the gospel message.

+ *Special assemblies.* Offer complete assemblies, planned by a local pastor or local Christian celebrity/athlete along with program staff, on four predetermined topics, with the aim of encouraging high school students toward the choice of sexual abstinence, school readiness, and other positive life-promoting choices.

+ *Parenting education.* Provide parents of participating public school youth with information and skills that promote family bonding and support systems.

+ *Youth Outreach Center.* A center can serve as a safe, positive neighborhood hub for a variety of spiritually based social and entertainment options, including an athletic league and summer program, as well as offering summer employment opportunities.

+ *High School Heroes.* This program showcases the strengths and talents of outstanding high school students by position-

ing them before junior high and elementary students as role
models for tutoring and assemblies.

• *Monthly principal meetings.* During a monthly breakfast, provide a forum for like-minded dialogue and strategy-planning
on improving the conditions within the schools, which also
includes a spiritual emphasis by a local pastor.

Technology and Education Institutes. This is a job readiness testing
and training center, which uses a variety of software applications to
teach and enhance marketable and academic skills through the following programs:

• *Adult literacy.* This program would teach basic reading and
writing skills to adults with little or no reading ability.

• *Pre-GED/GED preparation.* Such preparation provides the
necessary knowledge and test-taking skills to pass the state
examination.

• *Computer training.* In-depth, high-quality computer training can be made available in a variety of software applications, including Microsoft Office Suite, Adobe, Flash, and
HTML application training.

• *Professional development.* Promote personal development
and career advancement through providing useful skills and
knowledge.

Economic Growth Assistance. Seeks to provide a comprehensive approach to addressing the community's economic needs by helping the
unemployed and under-employed become employable. Such assistance
can have four components:

• *Job training.* This includes computer training, clerical training, and training in other job skills.

- *Networking.* Networking uses relationships within the business community to assist in job placement.
- *A business incubator.* A business incubator provides potential entrepreneurs assistance in every area of business start-up through compiling business plans, skills, and market assessments and more.
- *Junior statesmen and stateswomen.* This program is designed to prepare the next generation of political leaders, working in connection with the local political leaders.

Human Needs Assistance. Pressing issues limit community residents, including inadequate nutrition, joblessness, and housing and clothing needs. Local churches can assist individuals and families through the following services:

- *Food pantry.* When open to the public, a food pantry meets the needs of the community by supplying basic food items, such as sugar, oil, canned goods, and flour. The food pantry is stocked by donations from the church as well as community vendor donations.
- *Resale shop.* A resale shop provides local residents a place to purchase new and gently used items such as clothing, home accessories, and furniture at a highly discounted rate.
- *Housing assistance program.* This practical program offers seminars on credit repair, foreclosure prevention, home repair, home ownership, the US Department of Housing and Urban Development (HUD), and mortgage acquisitions.
- *Crisis intervention.* Such intervention provides counseling and crisis management assistance to those in immediate need through temporary assistance coupled with a long-term plan of moving the individual out of the crisis and into self-sufficiency.

- *Christ-giving.* This holiday event is designed for the distribution of food, clothing, and toys to needy families at Thanksgiving and Christmas, while also giving the opportunity for recipients to hear and respond to the gospel message.
- *Annual community health fair and job fair.* The health fair makes available health screening for breast cancer, prostate cancer, diabetes, high blood pressure, and many other health concerns free of charge to the local community semi-annually, while the job fair seeks to pair potential employers with qualified and trained employees from the community who have been assisted in résumé preparation and job skills acquisition.

Youth Programs. Such programs give youth an alternative to adult programming, with appropriate role models and vision casting. They include:

- *Summer programs.* Employ community youth in an established summer program hosted by your church that provides working parents with a place for their children to go that is safe, spiritually minded, and productive.
- *Sports leagues.* These leagues offer a natural place for mentoring by placing quality coaches in a position to interact with area and community youth through basketball or other sports leagues.
- *Local police involvement.* The church and local parents schedule a monthly meeting with your local police department to proactively address youth issues in the community.

Family-care pregnancy center. The goal is to assist girls and women to choose life for their unborn children, and ultimately for themselves, by aiding expectant mothers as they cope with the challenges of an unplanned pregnancy as well as other issues that affect their well-being. Also encourages fatherhood through mentoring and education of the baby's father. This is done through a host of services that include:

- *Medical services.* Services that can be offered include confidential pregnancy tests and sonograms; has a medical director and a registered nurse to oversee the medical services.
- *Family care education program.* Provides the expectant mother (and father) classes on topics such as prenatal care, childbirth, and newborn care. Regular workshops are available to those in need, covering areas affected by an unplanned pregnancy such as relationships, parenting, and spiritual growth.
- *Baby shop.* This allows girls and women to spend coupons earned from attending life-empowering workshops in order to cash in on basic necessities such as diapers and toiletries.
- *Counseling.* Lay and professional counseling can be provided, including information on sexually transmitted diseases, abortions, postnatal care, support groups, and vocational services.

These outreaches are not all-inclusive, and other programs and specific activities can be added too, but they give examples of activities geared toward the goal of establishing and nurturing relationships in the community, which then serve as a bridge back to the local church. Social ills cannot be solved simply with social helps, since their root is often spiritual in nature. These ministries exist to influence communities by meeting felt needs in such a way as to link the lost, hurt, and struggling with the body of Christ. The church then provides a new community offering discipleship, spiritual-growth opportunities, small groups, accountability, avenues for personal development, areas to exercise gifts through service, as well as relationships centered on Christ.

THE NATIONAL STRATEGY

The success of our local program inspired me to seek to replicate it in communities around our nation. Since every community has churches, schools, and families, our church has sought to create a training and networking program designed to equip and connect these churches with other like-minded churches across racial lines for the purpose of community transformation. I called this program the National Church Adopt-A-School Initiative (NCAASI), designing it to prepare urban and suburban churches across America to forge partnerships with public schools for improving the lives of urban youth and families.

Using our localized social outreach program as the model, NCAASI equips church staff, leaders, and volunteers with the knowledge and tools to build strong organizational and programmatic infrastructures to deliver effective social services in education, human needs, health, career development, and more.

Church and community leaders as well as lay leaders and members learn how to address human needs effectively while simultaneously modeling spiritual principles in a context of love, acceptance, and accountability. This then forms the relationships necessary for building the bridge that links them with the local church.

The primary goal is that of evangelism—seeking to bring the good news of Jesus Christ to those who have not yet responded to His offer of salvation. The gospel can be presented to anyone who chooses to come to the church as a result of the social services outreach ministry, or to receive training off-campus from the public school. Another goal is to incorporate those we serve into the life of the local church so that they can be discipled and become a functioning part of a body of believers who are operating under the rule of God. As individuals mature in their faith, they too can help others transform their lives.

A team of qualified servant leaders at The Urban Alternative (see

Appendix B) equips churches to embrace community impact through service. NCAASI does this through a variety of training options including on-site seminars, college or graduate level courses, and DVD-based lectures.

When churches operate properly under the kingdom agenda, progress and transformation occur naturally as the spiritual and social aspects of life work, positively affecting individuals, families, schools, and communities.

This model exists as a blueprint on how to apply the principles of the kingdom of God while meeting the needs of hurting people through caring interventions underlined with the message of hope. For more information, visit us online at ChurchAdoptaSchool.org or call 800-800-3222.

APPENDIX B:

The Urban Alternative

D r. Tony Evans and The Urban Alternative (TUA) **equip, empower, and unite** Christians to **impact** *individuals, families, churches,* and *communities* to restore hope and transform lives.

We believe the core cause of the problems we face in our personal lives, homes, churches, and society is a spiritual one; therefore, the only way to address them is spiritually. We've tried a political, a social, an economic, and even a religious agenda. It's time for a kingdom agenda—God's visible and comprehensive rule over every area of life because when we function as we were designed, there is a divine power that changes everything. It renews and restores is as the life of Christ is made manifest within our own. As we align ourselves under Him, there is an alignment that happens from deep within—where He brings about full restoration. It is an atmosphere that revives and makes whole.

As it impacts us, it impacts others—transforming every sphere of life in which we live. When each biblical sphere of life functions in accordance with God's Word, the outcomes are evangelism, discipleship, and community impact. As we learn how to govern ourselves under

God, we then transform the institutions of family, church, and society from a biblically based kingdom perspective. Where through Him, we are touching heaven and changing earth.

To achieve our goal we use a variety of strategies, methods, and resources for reaching and equipping as many people as possible.

BROADCAST MEDIA

Hundreds of thousands of individuals experience *The Alternative with Dr. Tony Evans* through the daily radio broadcast on nearly one thousand radio outlets and in over one hundred countries. The broadcast can also be seen on several television networks, and is viewable online at TonyEvans.org.

LEADERSHIP TRAINING

The Kingdom Agenda Pastors (KAP) provides a viable network for like-minded pastors who embrace the kingdom agenda philosophy. Pastors have the opportunity to go deeper with Dr. Tony Evans as they are given greater biblical knowledge, practical applications, and resources to impact individuals, families, churches, and communities. KAP welcomes senior and associate pastors of all churches.

The Kingdom Agenda Pastors' Summit progressively develops church leaders to meet the demands of the twenty-first century while maintaining the gospel message and the strategic position of the church. The summit introduces *intensive seminars, workshops,* and *resources,* addressing issues affecting the community, family, leadership, organizational health, and more.

Pastors' Wives Ministry, founded by Dr. Lois Evans, provides *counsel, encouragement,* and *spiritual resources* for pastors' wives as they serve with their husbands in the ministry. A primary focus of the ministry is the KAP Summit that offers senior pastors' wives a safe place to *reflect, renew,* and *relax* along with training in personal development, spiritual growth, and care for their emotional and physical well-being.

COMMUNITY IMPACT

National Church Adopt-A-School Initiative (NCAASI) prepares churches across the country to impact communities by using public schools as the primary vehicle for effecting positive social change in urban youth and families. Leaders of churches, school districts, faith-based organizations, and other nonprofit organizations are equipped with the knowledge and tools to *forge partnerships* and build *strong social service delivery systems.* This training is based on the comprehensive church-based community impact strategy conducted by Oak Cliff Bible Fellowship. It addresses such areas as economic development, education, housing, health revitalization, family renewal, and racial reconciliation. We also assist churches in tailoring the model to meet the specific needs of their communities while simultaneously addressing the spiritual and moral frame of reference.

RESOURCE DEVELOPMENT

We are fostering lifelong learning partnerships with the people we serve by providing a variety of published materials. We offer booklets, Bible studies, books, CDs, and DVDs to strengthen people in their walk with God and ministry to others.

* * *

For more information, a catalog of Dr. Tony Evans' ministry resources, and a complimentary copy of Dr. Evans' devotional newsletter,
call (800) 800-3222
or write TUA at P.O. Box 4000, Dallas TX 75208,
or log on to
*www.*TonyEvans.org

THE URBAN ALTERNATIVE

At The Urban Alternative, the national ministry of Dr. Tony Evans, we seek to restore hope and transform lives to reflect the values of the kingdom of God. Along with our community outreach initiative, leadership training and family and personal growth emphasis, Dr. Evans continues to minister to people from the pulpit to the heart as the relevant expositor with the powerful voice. Lives are touched both locally and abroad through our daily radio broadcast, weekly television ministry and internet access points.

PRESENTING AN
ALTERNATIVE TO:

COMMUNITY OUTREACH

Equipping leaders to engage public schools and communities with mentoring, family support services and a commitment to a brighter tomorrow.

LEADERSHIP TRAINING

Offering an exclusive opportunity for pastors and their wives to receive discipleship from Drs. Tony and Lois Evans and the TUA staff, along with networking opportunities, resources and encouragement.

FAMILY AND PERSONAL GROWTH

Strengthening homes and deepening spiritual lives through helpful resources that encourage hope and health for the glory of God.

TONYEVANS.ORG

THE LIFE UNDER GOD SERIES

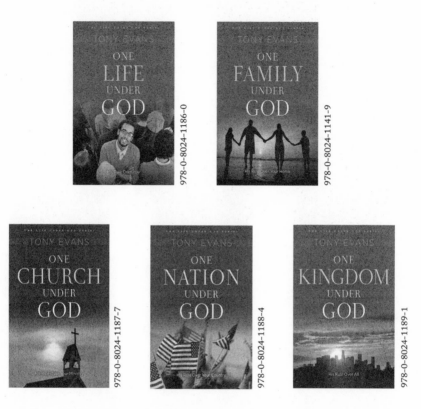

God's Word offers a biblically based kingdom agenda.
In The Life Under God series, Dr. Tony Evans highlights the five
areas that God has entrusted to us—personal, family, church,
and society—and demonstrates that Scripture has provided a clear
authority and a comprehensive approach to all of life.

MOODY
Publishers™
From the Word to Life

THE KINGDOM AGENDA

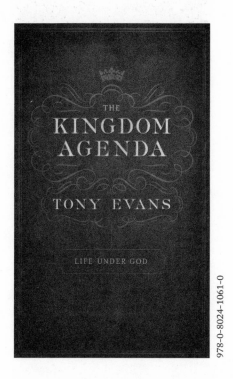

978-0-8024-1061-0

God's kingdom isn't just about theology and church. It isn't just a quaint religious idea or an obscure theological concept. It is about a whole new way of seeing the world and your place in it. As God's people, we are not limited by the choices this world offers us. God has an alternative plan for us— His kingdom with an all-encompassing agenda.

The Kingdom Agenda offers a fresh and powerful vision that will help you think differently about your life, your relationships, and your walk with God. When you start with a kingdom agenda, living in relationship with the true King and embracing your place in His Kingdom, nothing will ever be the same.

MOODY
Publishers™

From the Word to Life

MOODY
Radio™

*From the Word **to Life***

Moody Radio produces and delivers compelling programs filled with biblical insights and creative expressions of faith that help you take the next step in your relationship with Christ.

You can hear Moody Radio on 36 stations and more than 1,500 radio outlets across the U.S. and Canada. Or listen on your smartphone with the Moody Radio app!

www.moodyradio.org